Leadership
Sopranos
Style

HOW TO BECOME
A MORE EFFECTIVE BOSS

Deborrah Himsel

Dearborn™
Trade Publishing
A **Kaplan Professional** Company

Vice President and Publisher: Cynthia A. Zigmund
Acquisitions Editor: Jonathan Malysiak
Senior Managing Editor: Jack Kiburz
Interior Design: Lucy Jenkins
Cover Design: Design Solutions
Typesetting: Elizabeth Pitts

© 2004 by Deborrah Himsel

Published by Dearborn Trade Publishing
A Kaplan Professional Company

04 05 06 10 9 8 7 6 5 4 3 2 1

Library of Congress Cataloging-in-Publication Data

Himsel, Deborrah.
   Leadership Sopranos style : how to become a more effective boss /
Deborrah Himsel.
       p. cm.
Includes index.
      ISBN 0-7931-8150-X
   1. Supervision of employees. 2. Leadership. 3. Sopranos (Television
program) I. Title.
   HF5549.12.H56 2004
   658.4'092—dc22   2003016505

Advance Praise for *Leadership Sopranos Style*

"*Leadership Sopranos Style* contains valuable lessons about leadership that you won't learn in school and maybe not even on the job. Debbie Himsel is a true expert in the field of practical leadership techniques, and she shares her knowledge about what works—and what doesn't—in a funny, but seriously provocative examination of how to be a high-performing boss in the 21st century."
    —Andrea Jung, Chairman and CEO, Avon Products, Inc.

"*Leadership Sopranos Style* is a fun book. Debbie is an astute observer of practices of leadership. She distills the wisdom and the insights even from a medium that's entertainment. You will enjoy it, and many of the tips will be helpful to you."
    —Ram Charan, Author of *What the CEO Wants You to Know: Using Business Acumen to Understand How Your Company Really Works,* and Coauthor of the bestselling book, *Execution: The Discipline of Getting Things Done*

"*Leadership Sopranos Style* is a home run! It takes you through critical leadership concepts in a way that is direct, pragmatic, and entertaining. A refreshing and substantive read—the author knows business, knows leaders, and knows how to engage her audience."
    —Jean-Pierre Decosterd, President/CEO, Foods Division, The Americas Quest International

"A truly innovative book. Even if you've never seen the show, the book provides an entertaining way to understand the dynamics of a strong leader. Although most of us don't live in Tony's world, there are lessons about leadership that are definitely transferable. The book provides practical advice for real-world managers about how to be the best leader you can be."
    —Jill Kanin-Lovers, Senior Vice President, Human Resources and Workplace Management, Avon Products, Inc.

"Leaders recognize leaders. Debbie obviously recognized one in Tony Soprano. Besides the obvious 'he's the boss,' he demonstrates all the characteristics necessary of a great leader. He is charismatic with strong listening skills. He has the ability to lead with emotion and a 'tough love' style that is respected by all. And his communication style motivates people to listen to him and deliver the desired results. Debbie captures this in a way that is fun to learn and yet is very real. This is a great example of 'leaders are everywhere, you just have to look for them.' I truly admire Debbie's ability to 'connect the dots' with this show and leadership. I will watch *The Sopranos* with a very different ear and eye from this day forward."

—Lisa Berman, President and CEO, The Picture People, a Division of Hallmark

"If the mythical heroes and villains of folklore could be used to write books on leadership, why not a book on the leadership of Tony Soprano and his mob. Ignoring Tony's business ethics, this witty and well-written book is fun to read. Much can be learned from Tony's ten tough choices—his most challenging business decisions."

—Bernard M. Bass, Distinguished Professor Emeritus, Center for Leadership Studies, Binghamton University

"This is a unique and brilliant way to look at leadership."

—Stephen H. Rhinesmith, CDR International, Author of *A Manager's Guide to Globalization*

"*Leadership Sopranos Style* is what few books on this subject are today—simultaneously accessible, insightful, and instructive. From someone who has never watched *The Sopranos*, the description of this leader (Tony) is incredibly rich, finely detailed, and immensely entertaining. The lessons Debbie extracts from his character are powerful in their connection to tested theories and practical in their simple application to day-to-day life. This book has great relevance to all executives who want to improve their ability to 'get stuff done.' Tony is the perfect case study . . . but Debbie is the real leader here. Her ability to be direct and self-revealing about her own leadership journey, along with being innovative and courageous in writing a different kind of book on the topic, provides a great role model for all of us in this field. A great addition to the literature on leadership."

—Janet Spencer, Ph.D., Partner, Head of International Operations, Mercer Delta Consulting, LLC, and Coauthor of *Executive Teams*

DEDICATION

To Mom, Meem, and Pap, for your unconditional love and support

One of the questions posed by the vast literature on leadership is how, exactly, do leaders learn. Millions of dollars are spent each year on programs, seminars, workshops, and courses to help leaders acquire those qualities that will make them, and their organizations, successful. Companies develop elaborate strategies for providing the right combination of experiences and training that will fill their ranks with just the "right stuff." At the same time, there has been a lively debate over the years as to whether leaders are born or made. This is an interesting question, but ultimately irrelevant. As Peter Drucker once said, "There may be born leaders, but there surely are too few to depend on." In a complex, dynamic, and often apprehensive global environment, most organizations eagerly pursue ways to develop their leaders. It may not be possible to create a leader out of "whole cloth," but experience suggests that there are clearly ways to learn how to be more effective when you're at the top of the house.

The last few years have also seen a dramatic decline in respect for leaders. Former corporate icons have self-destructed because of their hubris, greed, and unprincipled actions. We question the skill of our political leaders and complain about the dearth of truly accomplished people who elect to pursue public office. While our cynicism and suspicions have mounted, there is still a deep desire in most of us to find people who are truly worth following. We maintain the myth of the "heroic" leader, someone who possesses near perfect qualities and has answers when we have only questions. Objectively, we know that leaders are afflicted by the same shortcomings we see in ourselves. But, myths die slowly, so our search continues.

Tony Soprano is no hero, and this book does not claim otherwise. This is not an attempt to canonize a fictional character whose accomplishments include "whacking" those who get in his way. This is hardly the advice we would give leaders to respond to competitive threats in their environment. And many of the tactics he employs to get results would land most of us in the slammer. Nevertheless, as this book demonstrates, there are valuable lessons that can be learned even from seriously flawed human beings—and not just about what they did wrong. If you reflect on those leaders who have fallen from grace, nearly all were at one time considered to be at the pinnacle of their professions. Would anyone doubt the talents of Martha Stewart, despite her recent troubles with accusations of insider trading? Or fail to acknowledge Bill Clinton's flirtation with greatness before his other flirtations got in the way? Ask contemporary leaders what shaped their views on how to lead, and they will tell you how much they were influenced by observing others in leadership positions—both their successes and their failures. That is the real point of this book.

How did Tony acquire his leadership skills? Certainly nothing in the series, or in this book, suggests that he attended any seminar to enhance his leadership effectiveness—as many thousands of executives do today. He's never participated in an off-site "bonding" experience with his team to improve their ability to work together. And there is nothing to suggest that Tony is, was, or ever will be a voracious consumer of leadership books. As a viewer of the series, I have trouble recalling any instance where he is seen even picking up a book. One presumes, then, that Tony's leadership skills are a combination of instincts and what he observed as he grew up on the mean streets of New Jersey.

Debbie Himsel is both a student and practitioner of leadership. She has studied the literature, worked with countless leaders to improve their effectiveness, and reflected deeply on the essence of true leadership. As this book demonstrates, she knows what she's talking about. She is able to extract from this popular, fictional character lessons that can be applied by almost anyone in a leadership position. She knows that leaders must be aware of their strengths and weaknesses, be able to articulate a clear direction for their organization, motivate their people, and put the right people in the right jobs. Whether you love him or hate him, agree with his tactics or not, there is little doubt that Tony Soprano has used these and other widely accepted leadership practices to achieve his success.

So I urge you to read this book. Even those who have not followed the series will find the connections that the author makes between Soprano's actions and conventional leadership practices to be insightful and witty. If you are a regular viewer, you will delight in recalling many of the episodes that have contributed to the enormous popularity of the series. This book is not only entertaining, but also it is relevant. My view is that learning about leadership can take many forms and is not restricted to attending a seminar or listening to the wisdom of the latest leadership guru. Some of the most valuable learning about leadership takes place in observing the actions of others and learning from their experience. This book provides the reader with the opportunity to look at a compelling fictional character through the lens of important leadership principles. There are clearly lessons to be learned from the likes of Tony Soprano.

Peter Cairo, Bearsville, New York (August 2003)

Contents

Acknowledgments

This book was purposely written as a very practical, nontheoretical book on leadership development. However, it is deeply rooted in leadership theory and close to 20 years of observation and practice in the field.

I learned the theory firsthand from some of the best in the business: Bernie Bass, Peter Cairo, Ram Charan, David Dotlich, Steve Rhinesmith, Noel Tichy, and Dave Ulrich.

I've observed extraordinary leadership firsthand from some of the finest leaders at both Pfizer and Avon Products, Inc. Andrea Jung, CEO of Avon Products, Inc., is one of the most charismatic and smartest leaders of her era. Her COO, Susan Kropf, is a role model of that rare combination of toughness, authenticity, and genuineness. Other gifted "teachers" from Pfizer and Avon include: Brian Connolly, Bob Corti, Harriet Edelman, Ben Gallina, Karen Katen, Hank McCrorie, Hank McKinnell, Amilcar Melendez, and Bob Toth.

I have also been fortunate to learn about leadership from some great bosses: Jill Kanin-Lovers, Ron Pannone, and Evelyn Rodstein. My mentor, Bill Pelton, provided leadership to his team as well as his wisdom to me.

Lastly, my best teachers have been those who have worked with me and for me. I continue to grow as a leader through their continued support and feedback. I thank them as well, especially my current team: Luli Bonorino, Robin Cohen, Mae Eng, Jonathan Fisch, Robin Fischer, Amy Greenholtz, Paige Ross, Diana Sacchi-Martinovic, Brenda Sanchez, Celeste Santos, Dan Schmidt, and my EQ coach, Alice DiPalermo.

Other colleagues who have influenced my thinking and may see their perils of wisdom sprinkled throughout this book include: Tom Barbieri, Rick Brandon, Jill Conner, Lee Ann Del Carpio, Charlotte Forbes, Mike Fruge, Ben Garcia, Neil Johnston, Blair Jones, Peggy McMahon, Agnes Mura, Donna Ng, Alice Portz, Lauren Powers, Ginny Pulos, Gail Robinson, Martin Snow, Janet Spencer, Wendy Weidenbaum, Ginny Whitelaw, and, of course, Jerri Frantzve.

Thank you to all who helped to shape the manuscript: Peter, Jerri, Jill, and Bruce. Also, a writer can never complete her task without an editing team. The team at Dearborn Trade has been a joy to work with. From the beginning, they have believed in this book and have been so supportive throughout the entire journey. A special thanks is extended to my editor, Jon Malysiak.

Writing a book while working full-time and teaching a graduate course at night was a little overwhelming at times. I am lucky to have an "infrastructure" of family and friends to help take care of me. Thank you to my mom, grandparents, Jane, James, Jim, Luisa, Jamie, Jeff, and Barbara.

Lastly, I live in Brooklyn, a place well known for its colorful mob characters. I had some help from a couple of guys from the neighborhood who know what really happens in the mob—thanks. You know who you are, and you made me promise no names!

Why Tony Soprano? What can any businessperson learn about leadership from a foul-mouthed, fictional mob boss? What relevance does the way Tony bullies and manipulates a small group of North Jersey mobsters have to do with managing a team, a division, or a corporation? Even if you can put aside what Tony does for a living, isn't his command-and-control style hopelessly out of date? Doesn't he use power when he should use influence and dictate when he should delegate?

I don't claim Tony Soprano is a perfect leader, and I acknowledge that he is a tragically flawed human being. I would argue, however, that he is a remarkably effective, empathetic boss who can teach MBAs a thing or two about leadership. Any fan of the television show will recognize the truth of this statement if he or she just reflects on how Tony runs his business. Think about the mutually accountable relationships he's established with his people, relationships in which members of his crew will literally lay down their lives to help him accomplish group goals. Consider Tony's charisma and how he employs it with Dale Carnegie–like verve to win friends and influence people. Recall his strategic brilliance as he diversifies his business, selectively taking risks that pay off in one new profit center after another.

Tony isn't the first person outside of the business community to be held up as a leader, nor will he be the last. Atilla the Hun, Jesus, General George S. Patton, and Machiavelli have all been the subject of leadership books for a reason. They force us to think about leadership in new ways, taking us out of our comfort zones and provoking us to consider alternative perspectives. People rightly complain that leadership models and theories don't work as perfectly in the real world as they do in textbooks, and

Tony provides us with a fresh model. This is an imperfect but highly realistic model, and I've found that it's one that resonates with all sorts of executives in many different types of businesses.

As a leadership-development executive at Avon, I'm always looking for new ways to help people learn and improve their skills. I use a variety of tools and techniques for this purpose, but the one that has really provided a breakthrough approach involves studying Tony Soprano's style, then interpreting and adapting it to a business environment. Part of the appeal of this style is that it gets results. Organizations today require leaders who know how to get things done, who are skilled at cutting through red tape and at finding innovative solutions to complex problems. These are examples of Tony's strengths, and grasping how he gets things done often inspires executives to come up with their own Tony-like approaches.

Another strength is his empathy. Companies need leaders who can build and maintain relationships with a diverse group of people. Despite Tony's bullying and biases, he is a deeply empathetic person who uses this empathy to create strong relationships within and outside of his organization. He's an active listener and a clear communicator, and he's not afraid to express his emotions. These are all highly prized leadership skills, and we can gain insight into how to use them by appreciating Tony's "moves."

Tony has other leadership strengths that I'll discuss at length, but his results orientation and empathy are certainly at the heart of his leadership gestalt. I came upon that gestalt simply by watching the show, and I'd like to share that experience with you and how I ended up using it in the workplace.

MORE THAN JUST ANOTHER PRETTY FACE

As I watched the first season of *The Sopranos* on HBO, I said on more than one occasion, "This guy [Tony] is actually a good leader." I made this remark with more than a little incredulity,

knowing I was ascribing effective leadership practices to someone who not only wasn't working in the corporate world but
who didn't actually exist! Still, things Tony said and did reso-
nated with me. His coaching challenges with Christopher re-
minded me of the struggles I had experienced with some of
my own people, and I admired the deft ways he resolved them.
His quest to gain self-awareness, too, struck me as something
many people in the business community could relate to. Increasingly, those of us in leadership development have seen the benefits for executives who become conscious of their strengths and
weaknesses; the people who learn how to manage their weaknesses become much more effective executives. Tony, like many
managers who come from traditional business backgrounds, was
reluctant to express or explore his feelings. His ability to overcome this reluctance—through his work with his own "executive
coach," Dr. Melfi—could serve as a guide for other businesspeo-
ple who were "raised" to keep their feelings hidden.

During the last episode of the first season, when Tony dis-
closes to his crew that he is seeing a psychiatrist, I began to think
seriously about the notion of Tony as a catalyst for leadership development. In this scene, Tony asks his crew to share their reac-
tions to his news about him seeing a therapist by "giving it to my
face." He went on to say that after they talked it out this one time,
it would never be discussed again. Brilliant, I thought. First, he's
soliciting feedback from his direct reports about a subject many
leaders would be loathe to discuss, giving his people permission
to be brutally honest about their feelings. Second, he's making
sure that this subject doesn't become a recurring and distracting
theme, insisting that this is their one and only chance to talk
about it.

I said to my family, "I wish I had the guts to do that with my
team." I had just received my 360-degree feedback report, and I
was working on an action plan but had not yet discussed anything
with my team. Perhaps, I thought, I should take my cue from Tony
and discuss my team's feedback directly with them rather than

just read what they had to say. The next day, I pulled out a flip chart and from my feedback report listed the top things that my team said I did well and the areas in which they thought I should improve. I brought in my team and gave them an overview of what we were going to do and told them they had 15 minutes to tell me everything they thought I should do differently. This was their chance. Instead of complaining to each other in the hallway or around the coffee machine about how I handled a given situation, they now had the opportunity to "give it to my face." Though I thought I had been open to feedback, I had never formalized the process and explicitly given them license to let me have it. At first they didn't say much, but shortly after the meeting began, they opened up. At the end of 15 minutes, they had said some things they had been keeping to themselves (it wasn't half as bad as what I had been expecting) and we had a game plan for moving forward.

During the first two seasons of the show, I found myself applying various lessons I learned from the series at work. For instance, I had always been the type of leader who at times shied away from giving direct feedback or confronting the tough issues. Though I was able to teach others how to do these things, I struggled with them myself, especially when I was dealing with people I cared about. I also feared that if I did not follow the feedback model correctly, I might inadvertently hurt someone. Watching Tony deliver feedback, though, taught me how being direct and honest with other people could be tremendously beneficial. Why did I have to watch my words so carefully? I should just spit it out in true Tony Soprano fashion. As I began giving more candid feedback, my worst nightmares did not come true. No one broke down and cried. No one said they hated me. No one resigned. In fact, the vast majority of people responded positively to the feedback and encouraged me to continue to be open and honest with my assessments and suggestions.

I also was impressed with how Tony stood up for himself and his people. I occasionally work with a consultant whose style is to attack when she doesn't agree with you; she is condescending and belittling, as well as extremely bright and quick-witted. In the past, I usually avoided engaging in debates with her. It seemed as if she was much easier to handle and less painful to deal with when I agreed with her. After watching Tony, though, I decided to try a different approach. Instead of allowing her attack, I challenged her point of view and explained why I thought she was wrong. I didn't do it with Tony's anger or fireworks, but I truly believed she was wrong and I let her know it. I'm not going to pretend that she liked my challenging her—she immediately became defensive and offensive (she attacked the basis of my challenge) simultaneously—but after talking about the issue for a few minutes, I could tell that she was at least willing to adjust her point of view if not change it to mine. It was a small triumph, but a triumph nonetheless. At the very least, it made me feel better that I had stood up and taken her on.

Up until this point, I had taught just about every coaching and feedback model on the market, all grounded in solid leadership theory. Tony helped me realize that there were other ways to communicate theoretical constructs; that he illustrated points about relationship building and strategic thinking without using fancy language. His actions conveyed volumes about what a good leader should do. I could point to something Tony had said or done, and people would get it instantly.

During season two, I began substituting Tony for five-step models. I tried out "Tonyisms"—quotes from Tony that related to leadership—in training courses with Avon leaders, and they responded enthusiastically. I used some Soprano examples in a coaching workshop, drawing parallels between how Tony dealt with situations that were similar to the ones they faced as managers. I noticed that many leaders, both men and women, seemed to relate to Tony's combination of power and vulnerability, the way his personal and professional lives overlapped, and how he grappled with decisions when there was no right answer.

I analyzed why Tony was such an effective teacher, talking to consultants, professors, and my colleagues about what made his responses to challenging situations so instructive for business-people. I concluded that a lot had to do with his almost mythical boss status and the hyperbole that goes with the television territory. James Gandolfini is a terrific actor, the character is incredibly well written, and the combination causes us to see leadership issues cleanly. When we read case histories about leaders—CEOs and other business executives—we get caught up in the details of the case and the leadership issues become cloudy. We can't judge or learn from a business leader's actions because we're thinking about the company's history, the factors influencing the industry, the competitive framework, and so on. When we watch Tony, we're not distracted by the business context. We can concentrate on how he solves difficult problems, communicates complex issues clearly, and creates innovative business concepts. And he makes it look easy. Instead of struggling to gain knowledge from a 100-page case history or to grasp complex leadership theory, we can simply look at what Tony did and say, "Oh, so that's how it works."

I'm not suggesting that Tony has the answer for every problem leaders face or that simpler is always better. It's just that this fictional character offers insights about leadership effectiveness faster and more dramatically than some of the standard development techniques organizations rely on. To that end, let's look at what happens when we put Tony to work in organizations.

WHEN THIS BOSS TALKS, PEOPLE LISTEN

One of the teams I was working with was struggling with how to become more cohesive and communicate more effectively with each other. We had not been making much progress, and during a break I remembered an episode I had recently seen in which Tony and his crew analyzed the problems being experienced by another crew while dining on macaroni and drinking wine. I also remembered that this seemed to be a technique Tony used when he wanted to facilitate a more open-ended problem-solving session; that the food and drink helped relax everyone and allowed them to exchange ideas more freely; that the frequent social interactions established a camaraderie that benefited the group's work process.

What if the team I was working with left the office building and met at a restaurant where we could eat, drink, and talk? I raised the prospect of all of us going out to lunch together, and everyone immediately protested they no longer had time to go out for extended lunches. This team had been under a great deal of stress in the past year, and most of them ate lunch at their desks to save time. As we talked, it became clear that they were having trouble with cohesiveness and communication in part because they no longer socialized much—they had gotten out of the habit of eating together or meeting after work for drinks. Making an effort to become more sociable became the key to solving the team's communication problems. I coached the leader of this team to preside over the group lunches much as Tony orchestrated his crew's meals, and I saw the bonds that had existed between team members in the past start to re-form as they joked, told stories, and expressed their feelings about what was happening in the company.

A few months later, I was attending a management meeting where a senior leader suggested that we needed a mechanism to surface conflicts and resolve them. We had recently reorganized a part of the operation and had realized that because of a complex but necessary matrix-reporting relationship, we were lacking a device to deal with the inevitable conflicts that would arise. After debating about and dismissing various conflict-resolution tools as inappropriate for this situation, we remained stymied until Tony came to the rescue again. When a conflict occurs in Tony's world, bosses call sit-downs. These sit-downs follow very specific protocols (which I'll describe in detail in Chapter 3), and can be very useful in encouraging people to talk about sensitive subjects and resolve complex problems. We figured out a way of adapting the sit-down methodology to meet some of the company's conflict-management requirements.

During the past few years, I've translated a number of different techniques and processes from the television show to use in my coaching and development work that I'll share with you throughout the book. *Translated* is the key word. Obviously, many of the methods Tony uses to achieve his family's goals are illegal or inappropriate to use in a corporate setting. Paying off an elected official to make a deal work isn't the way things are handled (though I suppose you might find those who dispute this last statement). As much as you might want to encase a lazy vendor's feet in cement and dump him in a Jersey swamp, that's not the way to establish good supplier relationships.

Translating, therefore, means using Tony's methods as inspiration for similar organizational methods. As you'll discover, Tony's direct, empathetic, and impactful communication methods yield a number of viable techniques that can be applied by any leader in any organization. The stories behind his decision-making approach—from the way he decides to kill Pussy to his choice to allow Junior the illusion of power—provide us with case histories that are worthy of study. By analyzing them, we can gain insights into effective decision making.

If you're at all skeptical about this premise—that you can learn about leadership from Tony Soprano—then I'd invite you to answer the following questions. After looking them over, I would bet that *Leadership Sopranos Style* makes more intuitive sense:

1. Wouldn't it be nice to have Tony Soprano talk to a talented but lone-wolf direct report who resists your efforts to get him to work as part of the team?
2. If your company had problems with liquidity, wouldn't Tony be a good candidate to help you arrange some loans?

3. If you needed to hire someone for an executive position who combines an ability to get things accomplished with an empathetic nature, wouldn't Tony be at the top of your list?

4. If you were facing a tough negotiation with a valued partner, wouldn't you want Tony on your team hammering out a win-win agreement?

5. Consider trying to recruit a young high performer from another organization who is being hotly pursued by other companies. Don't you think Tony would have more success than others, making this high performer an offer he couldn't refuse?

6. You're in danger of losing a top performer who is being wooed by headhunters and other organizations. Wouldn't this person be less likely to leave if his boss were someone like Tony who inspires great loyalty and respect from his people?

7. If you needed someone to launch a new moneymaking business fast, wouldn't Tony be your man?

8. Your board of directors is concerned about the company's downturn in recent months. They call your CEO on the carpet, and he assures them that he's going to turn things around soon. Do you think the board would attach more credence to this promise from your CEO or if it came from Tony's lips?

9. Wouldn't Tony ensure that meetings were conducted with great speed and efficiency; wouldn't he guarantee that core issues were addressed without preamble and pontification?

10. Wouldn't it be great to have Tony work with your CFO to deal with that accounts-receivable problem?

KEY PLAYERS IN TONY SOPRANO'S ORGANIZATION

I'm assuming that most of you are familiar with the names I've been dropping. Even if you've never watched the show, Tony Soprano's name has been in the news more than the name of any real-life mob boss. Still, I thought it would be worthwhile to provide you with a list of the names and identifying descriptions of the key people on the show. As you'll see, I've also included my interpretation of some of their roles and what their equivalent titles might be if they worked in a more traditional organization:

- **Tony Soprano**—COO of North Jersey mob family. Self-described captain of industry. May be COO, but really runs things.
- **Corrado "Junior" Soprano**—CEO of North Jersey mob family and also Tony's uncle. An old school family head, he is a traditional command-and-control leader whose methods and style seem hopelessly mired in the past.
- **Dr. Jennifer Melfi**—Tony's psychiatrist. Would make a terrific executive coach.
- **Christopher Moltisanti**—Tony's backup, nephew, and heir apparent. He may not be ready to run the family and may need some further seasoning, but he's blood. The equivalent of a hotshot sales or marketing manager at a major corporation.
- **Silvio Dante**—Consigliere or counselor to Tony and master facilitator of sit-downs. In-house general counsel.
- **Paulie Walnuts**—Tony's number two guy. He's a captain but feels underappreciated by Tony. Would likely be in human resources.
- **Herman "Hesh" Rabkin**—External advisor to Tony. Played the same role with Tony's father. Management consultant with a boutique firm.
- **Big Pussy Bonpensiero**—Former top soldier in the family. He paid the ultimate price for organization disloyalty and

now swims with the fishes. Downsized manufacturing executive.

- **Artie Bucco**—He owns the restaurant, Vesuvios, where Tony and his crew hold their regular meetings. He is a childhood friend of Tony and sees Tony as his mentor. Would be an event planner.
- **Richie Aprile**—Disgruntled employee. Returned from a prison stint to reclaim his previous position. Has disappeared. Richie would have been a middle manager.
- **Furio Giunta**—Outside talent that Tony recruited from his Italian business partners. He provides the muscle. Global marketing executive.
- **Ralph Cifaretto**—One of Tony's captains and a top earner. He's volatile and has been given feedback on his questionable judgment. Downsized out of a job. Equivalent corporate position: star salesman.
- **Gigi Cestone**—One of Tony's former captains. Gigi's promotion was not one of Tony's best decisions.
- **Johnny Sack**—COO of the New York mob family and business partner of Tony. He's also a leadership rival to Tony.
- **Carmine Lupertazzi**—CEO of the New York mob family. Old school. May soon be "acquired" by the New Jersey family.
- **Assemblyman Ronald Zellman**—Key business partner in many of Tony's schemes. He rarely meets a deal he doesn't like.
- **Carmela Soprano**—Tony's major alliance partner and his wife.
- **Meadow Soprano**—Tony's college-age daughter. Book-smart but low on business acumen. Likes to spend Daddy's money.
- **AJ Soprano**—Tony's adolescent son. Most likely does not wish to get into the family business.
- **Livia Soprano**—Tony's mother. The epitome of distrust and cynicism. Tried to serve as Junior's counsel from time to time.

ACTION-PACKED STORIES AND ACTION-ORIENTED EXERCISES

Whether you're a CEO or a young executive just starting out on the leadership track, this book will provide you with usable ideas and techniques. Some of them will be embedded in stories, both from *The Sopranos* and from organizational life. Others will take the form of quizzes, checklists, and role-playing scenarios.

I've also tried to make this book as readable and as entertaining as possible, and I would be remiss if I turned this into a dull lecture about leadership. As you might already have gathered, certain points can be made with tongue firmly planted in cheek; humor is not only entertaining but it sometimes helps make points more powerfully than a deadly serious sentence. Of course, Tony is deadly serious about some matters, and so am I—at least when it comes to helping people become more effective bosses. Throughout my career, I've been open to exploring alternative leadership-development methods that work better than traditional approaches. This is one alternative that I fully endorse.

The subject matter of this book runs the gamut. Strategy, structure, decision making, and conflict resolution are some of the topics covered, though I'll cover them in ways you might not have experienced. I'll also look at how to use charisma as a leadership tool and how to give and receive feedback in ways you might never have given or received it in the past. If you're an avid watcher of the television show, you'll find references to some of your favorite episodes, scenes, and characters. But even if you've never watched the show, you'll find that you'll quickly get to know the plot points and main characters and that the leadership lessons will be just as effective and relevant.

I want to emphasize that this is a book about leadership first and *The Sopranos* second. I am not a television critic. If you want to find detailed summaries of every show and discuss whether Tony will get back together with Carmela, then there are plenty of Web sites you can visit. My area of expertise is leadership development, and as a fan of the show, I discovered an astonishing synergy when combining summaries of Tony's moves and methods with the leadership problems and opportunities people are facing in organizations today. I realize that this is an unlikely synergy. I'm sure I would react skeptically if I heard about a book called *Bart Simpson on Leadership* or *The Leadership Secrets of Ally McBeal.* Nonetheless, I have a great deal of evidence that tells me that Tony's leadership style can inspire effective leadership development for all levels of executives.

Throughout the book, I've embedded Soprano-style nuggets of leadership wisdom. Some of them take the form of boxed "Tonyisms," quotes from Tony that I've used to illustrate leadership issues (and sometimes to provide comic relief from the overly serious, traditional way of viewing leadership). You'll also find "Tony's Ahas," one-sentence leadership lesson summaries at the end of each chapter. I've tried to crystallize each lesson into a sentence that Tony might whisper in your ear and cause you to say, "Aha, I get it!" During my own process of watching the show and testing what I learned in a corporate setting, these ahas gradually came to me. At first, I may have had doubts and suspicions about some of the Tony-inspired leadership lessons, but over time, everything came together, and I was able to see how Tony's style could be translated into a leadership development context. I hope you'll appreciate these small epiphanies as much as I have.

Finally, I would be remiss if I didn't return to an earlier point about the nature of Tony's business, especially in an age when the average person's distrust of corporations and leaders is high. Some people might say that the last thing the business world needs is for an author to hold up Tony Soprano as a paragon of leadership virtue. In fact, when one of my good friends heard about the book from my mother, her response was, "So, is that what Debbie is trying to do, turn us into little mafiosos?" Of course not. I don't condone illegal acts whether they're performed by mobsters or managers. I expect that readers, like the people who I coach and work with, are sophisticated enough that they'll realize my endorsement of Tony's leadership style is literally that—it's the style, not the substance. Anyone who tried to pull off the types of scams and schemes that Tony regularly uses would be immediately dismissed from any organization. On the other hand, if you can get past the terrible things Tony does and see the methods and moxie behind them, you can learn a lot about leadership. Tony's hopes and fears, dreams and demons, aren't much different from those of any leader. He faces the same issues as any executive—recruiting and keeping top talent, promotion decisions, global marketplace opportunities, financial crises—but he has a knack for handling these issues with uncanny skill. Tony also has flaws like any leader, and we can learn a lot by identifying his weaknesses and analyzing his mistakes. He makes the concept of leadership accessible. Tony's leadership potential, like that of many business leaders, is limited only by his failure to manage his vulnerabilities. Over the years, Tony grows as a leader because he becomes more aware of his shadow side. Watching him struggle to control these weaknesses—and sometimes failing in the attempt—is tremendously instructive. We can identify with Tony's struggles to control his fiery temper and bullying tendencies, and the more we see aspects of ourselves in Tony's struggle, the more we pay attention to how he handles his flaws.

Yes, all this is a work of fiction rather than fact. But like all good fiction, it provokes the audience to examine ideas that it might never have examined before. It asks us to examine the motivations and methods of Tony Soprano, and in so doing, it rewards us with inspiration and insight for our efforts.

As you might guess, I didn't want to write a typical book on leadership. It's not that I don't embrace leadership theory. I've spent almost 20 years in the field and everything I do and teach on this subject has its foundation in theory. But I've seen how people's eyes glaze over when they start reading articles and books that are heavy on theory and light on application, and I wanted this book to be fun and accessible. Surprisingly, perhaps, many of Tony's strategies and tactics are right in line with leadership theory, so the underlying messages are often similar. It's just more enjoyable to watch how Tony resolves conflict than it is to read chapter and verse about the conceptual underpinnings of a conflict-resolution approach.

At this point in your career, you've probably encountered numerous leadership approaches and models, and you've said to yourself: The theory is great, but it would be hard to put it into practice. Tony Soprano is nothing if not a pragmatist, and in the following pages, you'll find ideas about leadership that are amazingly useful in the rough-and-tough, cutthroat competitive world of business.

1

THE STRATEGIC GOAL IS TO MAKE SHITLOADS OF MONEY

If you want to be a more effective boss and a more effective leader, then you had better become a more effective strategist. The fastest way to rise to the top of an organization is by creating and implementing great business plans. The same principle holds true in Tony's organization. Have you ever wondered why Tony is a boss? Other members of his family may be more intelligent and more polished, yet Tony is the chosen one, and it's not just because of his Uncle Junior.

Even before you heard of this book, you probably tagged Tony as a leader. He's decisive, charismatic, and savvy. But what really sets Tony apart as a leader is his strategic acumen. Not only does he understand how to create a terrific business plan but he knows how to create one that works. Many times, CEOs and other executives are brilliant at crafting visions of the future for their companies and selling everyone on these visions. Their eloquent presentations of these strategies make them seem brilliant. Unfortunately, the strategies often possess only surface brilliance. They sound great, but they simply can't be implemented or they contain fatal flaws or they do not provide answers for possible changes in the marketplace.

Tony's genius is in coming up with eminently implementable business plans. Unlike highly creative but highly impractical strategies, Tony's plans don't require herculean efforts on the part of his people or demand huge financial investments. Instead, they're designed to be put into motion by ordinary people, and to be able to overcome obstacles that might hamper their effectiveness. Tony creates the right business plan for the right market at the right time, and that's what makes him such a great strategic leader.

Though Tony is smart enough not to put this business plan in writing, I've taken the liberty of putting my interpretation of it down on paper so that you can get a sense of its scope and solid foundation:

OVERVIEW OF THE BUSINESS PLAN
FOR THE SOPRANO FAMILY

Our overall goal is to make as much money as we can with as little risk (no jail time) through a diverse portfolio of operations consisting of legal and illegal business. Our net profits for the year are projected to be $4 million. We will reserve $500,000 for possible legal fees.

We have a multipronged strategy focused on:

- Ensuring cost-effectiveness of our current operations (for example, expense reduction at the Bada Bing!)
- Diversifying our portfolio into several business lines (legit and non-legit)
- Increasing productivity of our current customer base (for instance, larger loans for gamblers, pushing betting on multiple sports versus just on a single sport)
- Accelerating growth by acquiring new customers with new schemes
- Accelerating growth through alliances and joint ventures

I. OUR LINES OF BUSINESS—ONGOING OPERATIONS

Legitimate Profits (15%)

- Bada Bing! strip club
- Talent Management and Talent Brokering
- Barone Sanitation
- Satriale's Pork Store
- Garden State Carting

Construction (20%)

- Newark Esplanade ($300-million job)—no-show jobs
- Other potential jobs are currently out to bid.

Loan-Sharking (20%)

(Our loans are at a higher percentage than the bank. But if the bank would lend you the money, why would you need us?)

Gambling (20%)

- Card games
- Executive poker game
- Bookmaking

Theft and Fencing (10%)

- Regular truck hijackings and fencing of goods (Pokemon cards, clothing, electronics, etc.)
- Car theft—cars sold to our partners in Italy
- Safes, strongboxes, other people's scores (for example, the hit on the Colombians)
- Looting from construction sites (tiles, fiber-optic lines, etc.)
- First-run movie video and CD copies

Kickbacks and Protection (includes taxes from Hesh and others) (5%)

- Kickbacks, well, that's our piece of the action. It could be a commission on a contract or a payment to us so your business doesn't get interrupted.

- Some neighborhoods are a little rough, and business owners need protection. We also offer our "customers" protection from possible competitive threats.

Other Schemes (10%)

- Phone-card scam
- HUD housing scam
- Stock schemes
- Bust-outs (for instance, Davey's Sporting Goods Store, where we gain control of an established business and use its line of credit to buy other goods that are then sold through other means, while the business goes into bankruptcy)

Note: I do not condone drug dealing.

II.   SUMMARY STRENGTHS, WEAKNESSES, OPPORTUNITIES, THREATS (SWOT) ANALYSIS

Strengths:

- Diversification
- Strong cash flow

Weaknesses:

- Soft economy puts dent in our gambling operation
- Skills to oversee Esplanade project (Ralph is MIA)

Opportunities:

- Continued buildup of the Newark waterfront. May be other opportunities here.
- Soft economy creates more demand for phone cards, "discount goods," etc.

Threats:

- Aggressiveness of FBI. Who may have flipped now?
- Is Johnny Sack setting up to make a move?
- Junior is back. What will this mean for us?

III. OUR CUSTOMERS

- Suckers who will fall for our schemes
- Gamblers (low and high rollers)
- People who want to buy top of the line products for less and don't care how they acquire the products
- People who want to make money any way they can
- Men who want sex

IV. OUR COMPETITION

- We own our part of Jersey. Our competitive advantage is that we are large. We have the capital to support our customer base.
- We have a partnership agreement with a potential competitor, New York.
- We forge alliances with potential competitors (see later section).
- We forge alliances with others who can help us (Assemblyman Zellman, police officers, Reverend James Jr., etc.).

V. OUR MARKETING PLAN

- For our existing customers, we will continue to provide them with top-rate card games, betting opportunities, quality products, entertainment, protection, and access to ready cash. A lot of our business is through word of mouth so service is important to us. For example, the Bada Bing! is known for having the best and most curvaceous dancers. They are also pleasant to the customers. We make our money through our loyal repeat customers.
- We will seek new customers through relationships. Who can talk to which high roller? Who do we know who needs money or is in over his head? We are proactively seeking new customers in the loan-sharking business. If we think a customer can afford to borrow a little more, we may gently suggest it. We are also aggressive at seeing which businesses need protection. When a new business opens, one of the guys is the first to be on its doorstep.

- One of our hallmarks is that our shy business is buttoned up. We are aggressive at collecting past-due debts. We are known for not taking any excuses or letting people slide, even our friends. That's where Furio comes in. Brought over from Italy, he's the enforcer. The word on the street is that no one wants him knocking at their door. We are, however, flexible in alternative payment arrangements. For example, if you can't pay, we will take over your business and do what we call a "bust-out." It's not pretty, but it's better than dying.

- We actively seek alliances. Race or ethnicity does not matter. We have alliances with Jews, Russians, our extended family in Italy, and even American Indians. All that matters is that you can be trusted. For our alliance partners, we can be trusted to deliver on our agreements. We will not double-cross you.

- We seek growth by developing new schemes. Our target is to develop a new scheme every two months. We have a network of relationships and people who we can draw on quickly to make these schemes work. When we have a new scheme, we outline it ourselves, identify whom we need to partner with, work through our network of relationships to help set it up, and then pitch the idea. After that we are ready to go. The team is hands-on and we monitor the scheme to ensure its success, especially the first time around. The individuals we partner with on these deals know we will play fair with them, execute flawlessly, and give them their rightful take. We also keep our mouths shut and don't compromise their positions.

VI. OPERATIONAL PLAN

We will execute our plan through our crews led by our captains. Each crew has a clearly defined territory, as well as a business area of responsibility. Operations are coordinated through the capos.

Our base of operations is at the Bada Bing!, but we can often be found at Satriale's Pork Store or sometimes at the Crazy Horse.

Our primary mode of operation is through our muscle. We are known to have some of the best muscle in the tri-state area.

VII. SOCIAL RESPONSIBILITY

Our family has always felt that giving back to the community is an important and admirable goal. Each year we hold a Christmas party for the less fortunate kids in the area. Our Santa Claus (It used to be Pussy—God rest his soul!) delivers presents (we actually buy them).

We also do our part to protect our heritage and our good name. For example, we partnered with the Mohawk Indian tribe to organize support to protect the good name of Christopher Columbus.

VIII. CONTROLS AND REPORTING

We have rigorous financial controls in place: The capos and Patsy keep track of the money coming in and going out. If anyone gets out of line, they have to answer to Tony.

IX. TOP MANAGEMENT TEAM

- CEO—Corrado "Junior" Soprano (in name only)
- Underboss—Tony Soprano (really calls the shots)
- Consigliere—Silvio Dante
- Capo—Paulie Walnuts
- Accountant—Patsy Parisi

THE SECRETS BEHIND TONY'S STRATEGIC BRILLIANCE

Granted, you can't create a strategy that enters into highly lucrative but illegal businesses. You can, however, adopt elements of Tony's strategic thinking that should prove effective in any business. Let's look at the key elements of his plan.

Keep a Money Mind-Set

It's all too easy for business executives—especially executives in large organizations—to forget that their strategies must turn a profit. Insulated from the day-to-day operations, these executives often get caught up in "high-level" strategic thinking, creating elegant business plans that might earn them an A in business school but don't provide immediate revenue. Certainly, they understand the importance of making a profit, but they justify their strategies to themselves and others with talk of long-term profits and of getting a foot in the door of an emerging market. All this is fine, but, as Tony knows, if you don't meet the daily nut, someone will turn the screws on you.

TONY ON THE IMPORTANCE OF GOOD PROFIT MARGINS

"Sil runs the most profitable
strip club in North Jersey."

Tony's strategic philosophy is to think constantly about novel ways to make money. As part of his philosophy, Tony's focus is on how to maximize the spending capacity of his customer base. In other words, he always looks for a clever scheme to capitalize on the greed and other base desires of the human race. Tony encourages all his men to take responsibility for developing new ways to earn a buck. This does not always have to involve a big idea. It can be small ideas for a few thousand dollars. These add up just as easily.

The culture of Tony's crew is that it's everyone's job to come up with moneymaking schemes. In many companies today, this is often the job of a handful of people in the New Business group. Not too long ago, a senior leader with a large packaged-goods company told me he was talking with his people about a new strategy and one of his direct reports said they didn't have to spend time discussing strategic options because their New Business team would come up with them. The leader immediately explained that new business was everyone's role, but, clearly, this wasn't how this direct report and others in the company thought about it. Strategic thinking often isn't rewarded or motivated outside of a small group of people. Just as significantly, managers complain they don't have the time for creative, blue-sky thinking that results in viable strategies.

If you want to foster a money mind-set in your group, try the following Tony-like techniques.

Consistently talk about the need for fresh ideas. Fresh ideas can lead to profitable new ventures. Make a concerted effort to bring this subject up in formal meetings as well as in one-on-one conversations.

Reward your people. They deserve recognition not just for coming up with successful strategies but also for making strategic thinking a priority. Use everything from compliments to performance reviews and monetary incentives to demonstrate your desire for more moneymaking concepts and plans; make the money mind-set part of the culture so that people wake up thinking about new customers and new business.

Model the moneymaking mind-set. In other words, float your own trial balloons for various profitable ventures. Watch how Tony gets a glint in his eye when he thinks of a scheme and listen to the enthusiasm with which he presents it. Even if his scheme isn't viable, he clearly relishes talking about moneymaking ideas, and his enthusiasm for them is infectious.

Tap into the Most Compelling Customer Need

Tony's strategy revolves around the underlying needs of his customer base. That he has targeted customers who have baser needs than most is irrelevant from a strategic perspective. Tony takes the time to meet and talk with his customers as well as to talk to his people about their interaction with customers. This is Tony's version of focus groups and customer research. He pays acute attention to subtle shifts in customer requirements, always trying to stay one step ahead of the competition to remain on top. He searches for unmet customer needs, and when he finds them, he's quick to launch a strategy to capitalize. The customer focus that's key to total quality/process improvement/customer-centric initiatives would make perfect sense to Tony.

TONY ON MEETING KEY CUSTOMER NEEDS

"Garbage is our bread and butter."

For instance, Tony astutely analyzed the market of immigrants and determined that an unmet need was lower phone rates so they could call their families in the old country more frequently. As a result, he launched a telephone card scam that targeted immigrants in the New York City area. Similarly, Tony recognized that a market existed for designer label clothes that "fell off the truck." He saw an unmet need for designer labels among a certain amoral segment of the marketplace and again quickly capitalized on it. Tony pounces on markets where customers are highly motivated to buy, and this underlying strategic principle often results in fast and furious sales.

To develop this customer motivation focus, consider adopting the following tactics.

Look at familiar markets in unfamiliar ways. Certainly, Tony wasn't the first person to target immigrant and designer-label markets. Tony, though, viewed these markets from a different perspective. Like a good niche marketer, he avoided the saturated segments and concentrated on underserved segments. Instead of viewing your market head-on, rotate it in your mind so you're viewing it from a fresh vantage point. This means avoiding the mainstream customer approach and instead searching for what a smaller segment of the market needs but isn't getting. If everyone is selling on price to a given group, for instance, perhaps it means you need to meet that segment's desire for quality.

Get to know your customers on a first-name basis. People have always talked about the need to know their customers better, but it's still relatively rare for senior executives to spend significant amounts of time interacting with current and prospective customers. This means spending time in stores and online, asking questions of people and answering their questions. It means going beyond sitting in on a focus-group session. These are fine, but you must engage in customer dialogues if you want to come up with the type of strategies for handling unmet customer needs that Tony is so skilled at devising. Tony isn't afraid to ask customers for feedback or ask them the tough questions; he really wants to know what's on their minds. Knowing your customers on a first-name basis means knowing what's going on in their heads and not just what's taking place in their businesses.

Be observant. Tony sees all, knows all. At least that's how it appears. He is constantly studying situations and people, watching for entry points, for an edge. Too many leaders acquire the vast majority of their information secondhand. By being constantly vigilant and paying attention to everything that takes place around you, you can gain access to firsthand data.

Subtly Emphasize New Business over Old

This is a delicate balance, for you need to sustain and update the old while breaking new ground. While some companies err by focusing too much on the new—Procter & Gamble got in trouble because it neglected to adequately resource existing brands—the tendency is to nurture established winners rather than to explore uncertain opportunities. Tony grasps a great truth of leadership in the 21st century: If you want to do more than maintain your market share, you need to explore new business opportunities constantly. Through business-process reengineering, Six Sigma, downsizing, and a variety of other initiatives, most companies have squeezed about all they can from their operations. They've managed their supply chain as well as they can to obtain savings and achieved maximum cost reductions through integration. If they want to grow their companies, they recognize that new business is the answer.

Tony's approach—taking numerous small but acceptable risks to create successful new ventures—fits market realities in the early 21st century. In a time of great uncertainty and rapid change, it makes no sense to bet the house on one roll of the dice. If you try ten new ventures a year and only half of them pan out, you'll still be ahead of the game. Tony seems to come up with one new scheme per episode, and though some of them flop, enough work that he's able to keep profits high and losses low.

To adopt this new business strategy, employ the following tactics.

Make a commitment to generate at least one new business idea each week. You obviously aren't going to turn all these ideas into real businesses, but the commitment to generating ideas will shift your strategic thinking from maintenance to creation. To facilitate this process, think small and creative rather than big and me-too. Like Tony, look for market niches. Concentrate on market segments your competitors may have considered too small. Does your company already possess resources that can be used to create a new product or service quickly and relatively inexpensively?

Formalize regular new-business meetings. Make them part of your routine. These formalized meetings communicate to your people that you take this subject seriously and want them to actively participate in this process. It's critical, though, that you act on some of the ideas brought up in these meetings and reward those who initiated them. If it's all talk, your people will quickly realize this fact and devote little energy or creativity to develop new-business concepts. Make sure you choose the best ideas and take them to the next stages—funding, plan development, and implementation—to demonstrate your commitment.

Like Jack (and Tony), be nimble and quick. Tony launches new businesses with a minimum amount of fuss and bother. Though he has the advantage of more power and control than most CEOs possess as well as a smaller organization to operate, his skill at bypassing lengthy meetings and approval processes is one that more leaders need to emulate. I'm not suggesting ignoring organizational protocols as much as learning how to work the system so that great new ideas can be launched before they become stale old ideas. To a degree, this means being politically savvy, making the right connections, and taking some risks. If you want to be nimble and quick in launching new products and services, these skills are necessary.

Leverage Relationships and Networks

Tony's business is all done through relationships. For Tony, it is who knows whom and how can you leverage those contacts to get what you need from the right person. Tony is deliberate and calculating about his relationships. He maintains police, union, political, and business contacts regardless of ethnicity, race, and, yes, even gender (the lovely Annalisa in Naples). He works through granting favors, reciprocity, and cold cash.

Because so much depends on these relationships, Tony protects them like the precious things they are. For example, he launders his money through the Russian, Slava. When Christopher and Paulie got too physical with Valery, Slava's friend, Tony makes it clear to Paulie that if Slava makes the connection, it's his problem. He does not want to be associated with the attack on Valery because it could harm his Slava relationship. The ferocity with which Tony protects his relationships and networks demonstrates how essential they are to his strategy.

While corporate leaders value relationships and networks, they don't always view them as the strategic tools that Tony does. For many leaders, they remain tangential to their strategies, nice to have but far less important than the core ideas of the strategies themselves. In this traditional view, relationships are useful for supporting strategic initiatives. In Tony's view, they are what make these initiatives succeed or fail.

In any global business, leaders are learning to cultivate relationships and connect to networks to achieve their strategic goals. For instance, one organization was seeking to acquire a small or midsize firm in China, but it was targeting a group of companies that were family-owned and weren't actively interested in being bought. This U.S. organization learned that it couldn't achieve its strategic goal simply by offering a lot of money or by making convincing presentations. It discovered that the first and most important step involved working through a network of current relationships to make contact with the right people in the targeted group of Chinese companies. Only through this network did the company have a chance to start a productive dialogue with the head of one of the family-owned companies. Contrary to its previous experiences, this organization found that it had to nurture relationships rather than make an offer to achieve its goal.

To leverage relationships and networks, try the following.

Don't rule out untraditional networks or unlikely people. We all have our prejudices and preferences in these areas, as does Tony. Tony, however, rises above his biases for pragmatic business reasons. You may be biased against small companies that are only a fraction of your size or entrepreneurs who seem less than professional. You may find the experience of dealing with people in countries other than your own foreign in more ways than one. If so, you're artificially cutting yourself off from people who may be critical in making a strategy successful. In a global, interdependent world, organizations need to forge alliances with individuals and groups who they may never have even considered doing business with in the past. Be open-minded in evaluating prospective contacts and partners. Even small companies today can deliver a lot of know-how for the money.

Act like a networker rather than a delegator. Tony knows how to work a room and press the flesh. He could simply sit in his office and give orders à la Junior and the other bosses, but he realizes that the stronger his relationships are with a diverse group of people, the better position he's in to achieve his goals. Granted, not everyone has great networking skills, but it doesn't require much skill simply to be proactive when it comes to meeting a wide range of people. When you look at every trade show, every cocktail party, and every charitable function as an opportunity to network, then you're bound to form relationships that will dovetail with your strategic needs. I know an executive who makes a list of everyone he wants to meet before attending a trade show or conference, visualizing exactly who he needs to talk to and thus increasing the odds that he'll actually talk to them. As he meets each one, he methodically checks their names off the attendee list.

Seek Alliances and Joint Ventures with Those Who Share Your Goals and Values

More than one executive has told me that networking makes them uncomfortable, in part because they feel like a cold-calling salesperson who is exploiting every contact she's ever made. It's important to remember, though, that you don't create relationships with just anyone. It makes no sense to form partnerships with people who are unethical or who share different beliefs and values about business. While Tony is fearless in seeking alliances, he generally partners with others who share his business goals and his values of trust and loyalty. They may be very different from him in terms of their backgrounds and business styles, but the common goals and values cement the relationship.

Tony is good at identifying the gaps—the difference between the resources his crew possesses and the resources he requires to accomplish an objective—and creating alliances to fill these gaps. For example, when there was unrest with the joint-fitters union, he could have just muscled his way to a solution but, instead, he looked to "partner" with Reverend James Jr. to minimize the violence and thus reduce the risk. Reverend James Jr. shared Tony's goals and values, and thus it made sense to partner with him, even though the Reverend and Tony were polar opposites in certain respects.

To seek goal- and value-oriented alliances, you should do the following.

Be aboveboard with your goals for a partnership. Too often, executives don't show all their cards to their partners—especially when their partners are competitors or vendors and they're fearful of revealing "trade secrets." As a result, the two parties enter an alliance with different expectations of the results. Invariably, the alliance falls apart because of these differing expectations.

Communicate your goals early and clearly. Explain exactly what you want to get out of the partnership and make sure you understand what your prospective partner desires. If it seems like you're on the same wavelength, then a partnership may make sense.

Assess your prospective partner's values versus your own. This is a more difficult measurement than goals, for values tend to be less tangible. Still, even if you didn't know much about the prospective partner until recently, a few conversations can give you a sense of what's important to him in terms of trust, loyalty, honesty, accountability, and diligence. It would be great if you had Tony's laser-like perception and could quickly discern whether someone shared your values. Most people, though, can simply talk about the nuts and bolts of a possible working relationship to determine what the other person values. Is he willing to cut corners? Does he value speed over quality and results over values? Is he so cautious that he moves at a snail's pace, while you're willing to take certain risks to capitalize on opportunities? If there's a huge gap in what you both value, then building a relationship is a bad idea.

Focus Your Efforts on Execution

As good as Tony's strategic thinking is, his execution is even better. This is where many leaders and their companies fall short. They may spend time and money developing sound strategies but fail to pay attention to the details necessary for effective execution. In Tony's Webistics scheme, he figured out how to get the broker's license and set up an operation through a legitimate brokerage house and then he had Christopher supervise the two "brokers," Matt and Sean. Tony made sure he had the necessary resources and the adequate supervision to ensure that the scheme was carried out properly. Similarly, in Tony's HUD deal, he mapped out the plan, identified the talent needed to make it work, and then split the supervision between himself and Ralph to ensure that the plan was executed as he envisioned it. Tony even went so far as to drive over and look at the houses that were bought as part of the scheme. When he discovered that one of the buildings was a crack house, he leaned on the assemblyman to make sure the house was "cleaned up." Tony recognized that the crack house might create an obstacle, and his hands-on efforts cleared that obstacle.

TONY ON ASSESSING THE IMPACT OF
EXECUTING A STRATEGY

"What do I get if I whack Carmine?"

Tony gives orders, but he doesn't limit his involvement to issuing commands. In many instances, he'll become personally involved in making sure an order is carried out as he specified and he'll do what he can to help others achieve the results he wants. He realizes that the devil may be in the details. Too many leaders view execution as "beneath them." They deem developing a strategy worthy of their time, but the nitty-gritty details of implementing that strategy strike them as mundane. They may be great strategists, but their reputation is as poor strategists because something always seems to go wrong between the idea and the execution.

To make sure your strategic execution is as solid as your strategic thinking, you should do the following.

Get involved in some aspect of the implementation process. Realistically, you're not going to have time to visit your version of a crack house. If you're undertaking a major strategy, this endeavor may be occurring across a wide geographical territory and involve hundreds or even thousands of people. Still, no matter how massive a strategic initiative might be, you can be personally involved in rolling out some aspect of it. Whether it's a trip with your purchasing agent to supervise selection of a particular material or going online with your management information systems (MIS) person to beta-test new software, you can obtain a firsthand look at how your idea appears in the field. This is always a revealing process for the strategist because she knows the strategy better than anyone and is more likely to discern the glitches before anyone else or sense how a process should be tweaked. Therefore, make sure you have some implementation responsibility.

Be brutally honest in your assessment of what's needed to get things done. Don't fool yourself into thinking you have the resources you need or the time necessary to meet the deadline. Too often, strategists become so wrapped up in their visions that they convince themselves they can make their strategy happen through sheer force of will. This enthusiasm and idealism is useful for giving birth to the strategy, but it can be counterproductive once the strategy is fully formed and needs nurturing. Shortfalls in time, money, and people resources doom promising strategies, and you need to face facts about these shortfalls sooner rather than later. It's tough to admit that you don't have what you need to make a strategy work, but if you're like Tony, you'll exert your muscle or your charm to gather these resources preexecution.

Diversify Your Revenue Streams

When Tony was resisting giving Carmine and Johnny Sack a piece of his HUD deal, New York put a halt to the Esplanade project until this conflict was resolved. Because Tony was diversified in his businesses and Johnny Sack was not, Tony was able to wait out Carmine and Johnny until they were ready to negotiate the lower percentage cut that he thought was appropriate. His other operations continued to bring in money and give him a cushion that Carmine and Johnny lacked. In many ways, this is similar to some organizations that are diversified in several overseas markets, the theory being that one country's sales will compensate for another country's devalued currency.

From a strategic standpoint, some executives don't like diversifying revenue streams when one stream has been flowing swiftly and steadily for a sustained period of time. In the past, this may have made sense. Today, though, there's so much volatility that diversified revenue seems critical for most operations. Therefore, you should do the following.

Explore diversification options. Of course, this is easier said than done, but every leader owes it to his organization to at least investigate alternative revenue possibilities. This is a long-term goal, but smart leaders like Tony realize that they make themselves vulnerable when they lock into one revenue source. As wonderful as that source has been, the odds are that it won't continue to be wonderful indefinitely.

NOT YOUR AVERAGE STRATEGIST

As you review these strategic traits, you may be thinking that it's easier for someone like Tony to diversify his revenue streams, seek alliances with people who share his values, and keep a money mind-set. It's true that an individual who works for a smaller, private business and possesses a great deal of power will have an easier time of charting this type of strategic course. At the same time, however, I'm not suggesting you mimic Tony as much as that you draw inspiration from him. Too many leaders rely on textbook strategies, and these are not textbook times. My hope is that Tony will inspire you to leverage networks instead of going it alone or to focus your efforts on new business rather than just relying on the old cash cows. Short of hiring someone like Tony as a consultant—an interesting proposition—here's some Soprano-like advice to help you adhere to Tony's approach to building and expanding a business.

TONY'S STRATEGIC AHA!
Go for the money, but stick to your guns.

2

CHARISMA

More Than a Flashy Tie and a Cheap Cigar

From former General Electric head Jack Welch to former President Bill Clinton, certain leaders seem to possess a magical quality that serves them and their organizations well. It exaggerates their strengths and minimizes their weaknesses, surrounding them with an aura that becomes a type of protective shield. More than that, their charisma draws people toward them and creates instant loyalty and respect. Tony Soprano has charisma in spades.

But why? What does Tony do that generates this charisma? More to the point, what can you do to generate it? While you probably won't become a magnetic personality just by studying Tony's moves, you can create a style based on his example that will serve you well as a leader. You can learn to have "presence," the ability to command attention when you speak or even when you enter a room. This presence will enhance all your other leadership skills. To develop it, we need to understand what makes Tony so charismatic.

INNER STRENGTH AND
BELIEF TURNED OUTWARD

From the very first moment of Tony's television existence when he is sitting in Dr. Melfi's office, you are drawn to him. You sense immediately that there is something different about this man, both in terms of his physical strength and his strength of character. He fills a room, and people immediately notice him. Though his fat Cuban cigar is blowing smoke in everyone's face, no one would even think of asking Tony to smoke it elsewhere. Though Tony is a big man and in the mob, these aren't the only reasons people notice and respect him. It's the style with which he carries himself, the way it reflects his inner fire and emotional intelligence. He manages to project his inner beliefs and passions outward in a clear and convincing fashion.

TONY ON ANALYZING A COMPETITIVE THREAT
"Richie doesn't have the balls to
make a move against me."

His inner qualities emerge in various ways: the twinkle in his eyes when he finds something amusing, the deeply soulful look when he's empathizing, the aggressive body language when he's angry, and the clipped, staccato manner of speaking when he wants to make a key point. Tony doesn't do all this consciously. He's a rare "natural" leader, able to project his authentic self with great conviction and power. Tony's authentic self is contradictory. As the previous list of inner qualities suggests, he can be tough and soft, brutal and kind, ignorant and insightful.

Most people hide who they are, and this prevents the full strength of their character from emerging. Most individuals who harbor these contradictory impulses attempt to mute one side or both sides of themselves. If they're in leadership positions, they may not want to appear too empathetic for fear they'll be taken advantage of. They may also not want to be too outspoken or forceful for fear of turning people off.

Tony, though, embraces his contradictions. He's mature and childlike, strong and sensitive, accepting and prejudiced. The image of him walking down the driveway in his ratty bathrobe, unshaven and sloppy-looking, does not seem to mesh with the man who fought off two hit men with his bare hands. The man who cried when the ducks flew south for the winter doesn't jibe with the man who almost ran a deadbeat gambler over with his car in the parking lot of his office. Tony has an air of intrigue about him because of these contradictions, and people sense that he's someone special because of them.

I'm not suggesting that you should develop a contradictory style. You can, however, allow who you are and what you believe to shine through. The dictionary defines charisma as that special quality that gives an individual influence, charm, or inspiration over large numbers of people. If you learn how to communicate your special quality to others—as opposed to acting the part of a leader—then you can develop a certain amount of influence, charm, and inspiration. This doesn't mean all heads will turn toward you when you enter a room or you'll become a celebrity CEO who regularly appears on the covers of business magazines. What this means is that you can work at developing an authenticity as a leader that will enhance your career and your effectiveness.

WHAT WE CAN LEARN FROM TONY'S CHARISMATIC WAYS

Obviously, it would be silly for you to start acting like Tony, especially if your style has little in common with his. If you're an even-tempered, egalitarian executive and you were transformed into a belligerent, mercurial one, no one would buy this change for a minute. You'd have no more charisma than Tony's barber.

You can, however, learn a lot about how to create your own charisma by analyzing how Tony does it. Let's examine the four components of his charisma and how you can take advantage of them:

1. Strong beliefs and values relating to the work and "our thing"
2. Self-confidence and competence, balanced with authenticity
3. Strength and the perception of invincibility
4. Comfort with power

Strong Beliefs and Values Relating to the Work and "Our Thing"

Even though he is involved in illegal and basically immoral activities, Tony not only justifies his actions but also takes pride in them and sees "our thing" as serving a higher purpose. During Tony's discussions with Dr. Melfi, his belief in the rightness of his work comes through. She frequently challenges him about the business he's in and why he persists in being a criminal. His response demonstrates that he views what he does in a broader context than most people, that he sees it as something noble and even heroic. He told Dr. Melfi about the Italian immigrants who "took what they wanted." He went on to say that the immigrants ". . . weren't educated like the Americans. But we had the balls to take what we wanted." He talked further about how it was J. P. Morgan and the other bankers who were the real crooks.

If Tony didn't have a strong belief about what he did for a living and if he didn't value his work, his magnetism would diminish. He sees the Soprano family as part of a larger plan and having a higher purpose than just making money. Building a cohesive family based on trust and loyalty is the underpinning of Tony's ideology. Tony engenders so much respect from his people because of his unswerving belief in these higher values.

For example, when Christopher cavorts with Hollywood screenwriters and is being drawn into their world and away from the family, Tony senses that Christopher is forgetting who his real family is and what it stands for. At a party at Tony's house, Tony turns to Christopher and tells him that if he is not back in ten minutes, he should not return, adding that if he does come back, he will assume "that you have no other desire than to be with me and your actions will show me that every day." This belief-driven statement is far more charismatic than if Tony had said, "You better get back here in ten minutes. If you do, great, things will be fine."

At the ceremony when Christopher becomes a made man, Tony makes it clear that from now on, Christopher's loyalty is to the family. Everyone and everything else is secondary. He conveys that what's important to him—and what should be paramount to Christopher—are the codes of honor, family, and loyalty. In his way, Tony is a devout man, but his religion is his crime family and the tradition and beliefs that come with it.

When Tony becomes upset with Ralph for killing Tracee, a stripper, it isn't just because Ralph has done something stupid. In Tony's eyes, Ralph has violated the family's code. He has killed without purpose. Murdering someone—especially a woman—for no reason struck Tony as disrespectful not just of him, but of the organization and its values. Tony's antipathy toward Ralph is less because he's a killer and more because he's a killer who tramples on their family's shared values.

In 100 different ways, Tony communicates his fierce belief in these values. For most of his crew, Tony's devout nature is inspirational. He is like a religious leader for he seems to believe more fervently and know the beliefs better than anyone else. He has tapped into the essence of what the family is all about, and this elevates Tony in their eyes. Though this comparison may seem a stretch, Tony and Dr. Martin Luther King Jr. share the same eloquence about and passion for their "causes." That Dr. King's cause was significantly more noble than Tony's isn't the issue here. Both recognize that if a leader doesn't believe completely in what he is doing, he can't expect others to believe and follow.

Assuming you have strong beliefs and values relating to your organization and the work you do, you need to communicate this with consistency, clarity, and conviction. Here are some ways you can do so and tap into one source of Tony's charisma as a leader:

- Write a description of what you stand for as a leader. Why should your direct reports follow you? Are you driven to help your people grow and develop? Do you believe leaders should lead with equal amounts of compassion and authority? What are you passionate about in your organization; what in its tradition, culture, and approach to business do you want to uphold and pass on to others?

- List three ways you can translate what you stand for as a leader into words and actions. For instance, if you stand for "delivering results with integrity," one action you might list is "forming partnerships with vendors where we don't take unfair advantage of our position as the customer." The three things you list can be small actions or statements. One item on the list may be to talk to direct reports about how you don't want them to cross any ethical lines to meet performance goals; how you'd rather have them fail to meet these goals and maintain the ethical standards you've set.

- Practice putting at least one of these listed items into action. This may feel awkward at first. You may not be used to allowing your people, your customers, or your suppliers see your underlying values and beliefs. Motivate yourself with the image of Tony defending his belief in the mob culture to the death. If he can speak passionately about murder and mayhem, surely you can talk about results and integrity.

Self-Confidence and Competence, Balanced with Authenticity

Followers want a leader who expresses optimism, not doubt. There is something magical about a leader who radiates optimism and certainty that goals can be achieved. People want to work hard for this leader, convinced that their work won't be in vain. Tony is self-confident without being arrogant (at least most of the time). While this is a tough balance to achieve, Tony manages it, in part because he is so genuine that no one thinks that he's putting on airs. While Tony is tremendously self-assured about his own ideas and opinions, he also solicits other people's ideas and opinions and acts as if he really wants to hear them. When someone does a good job, he doesn't try and take credit for it; he's willing to acknowledge the hard work and insight of others. Unlike some leaders, Tony isn't so insecure that he feels compelled to remind everyone how good he is at his job. Most of the time, he lets his track record and the results he generates speak for themselves.

Though charisma is created from confidence, it's diminished by doubt. Tony rarely shows self-doubt, despite major setbacks, problems, and snafus. When Tony receives word that federal indictments were going to be announced soon that could wreak havoc in his organization, he doesn't panic. Instead, he encourages his people to focus on what they need to do to be productive and to proactively do their "spring cleaning." When it looked like Tony might be arrested and charged with murder, he doesn't betray any fear or doubt. Even when it looks like he might do some time for the illegal airline tickets that he gave to his mother, Tony remains optimistic.

In religion and politics, charismatic individuals walk through the streets and people are frantic to touch them. It's as if their wisdom and power might somehow rub off on those lucky enough to get close to them. The same is true of highly confident leaders. When times get tough, other people draw sustenance from them, and this quality adds to their charisma. Christopher frequently looks to Tony to boost him up when he's down, and Tony obliges, offering stories or even a few empathetic words to get Christopher back on track. When Gigi takes on the crew leadership and talks about all the stress he's under, Tony expresses confidence in his leadership and tells him he is doing a good job. Though Tony has high expectations for all his people, he also is confident that they can deliver on these expectations. More often than not, he pats them on the back and reassures them that they can meet the goals that have been set.

Competence forms the foundation of an individual's self-confidence and how he is perceived. It's not enough to look the part; you need the knowledge and skills to back it up. Without competence, even the most glib and eloquent leader eventually proves to be a fraud. What seems to be charisma turns out to be nothing more than flamboyance. Followers want a leader who knows what he's doing. The stories of how Tony's expertise helped him rise through the ranks are legendary. Tony is a great earner in large part because he's a great idea man; he is skilled at creating novel moneymaking schemes. The HMO and HUD scams were Tony's inventions. He is an out-of-the-box thinker, and his people love the excitement and daring of his schemes. Tony is competent not only because of his consistently profitable ideas but because he's never been to prison. His skill at avoiding jail is much admired by his crew and inspires them to take risks they might not otherwise take.

Tony's authenticity goes hand in hand with competence and confidence. Without his genuine quality, Tony is just another smart mob boss. With it, he's not only smart but special. It separates him from the mob. Watch how Tony maintains eye contact when he speaks with someone. When he has something important to say to an individual, that person feels like he's been singled out for special attention. His whole body language conveys his genuine interest and attention. When he's engaged in an important conversation, he moves closer to the other person, his gestures are more animated, and his voice and gaze grow more intense. Tony also asks a lot of questions, more than most leaders are willing to ask (for fear of showing they don't know everything). And, finally, Tony knows how to have fun. Many leaders feel they must preserve their dignity by remaining aloof; they don't go with the troops to have a drink or watch a sporting event or attend a party. Tony is more than willing to let his hair down. He likes nothing better than a good time, and his crew appreciates his willingness to be "one of them." With Tony, what you see is what you get.

TONY ON ACKNOWLEDGING FAILURE

"I know what happened was wrong.
I'm an asshole. It won't happen again."

There are numerous examples of Tony's down-to-earth nature. When he is helping AJ change a tire, AJ suggests that Tony call the auto club and Tony replies, "We change tires in this household." His next-door neighbor, Dr. Cusamano, and his friends invite Tony to their club for a round of golf. As they talk about the stock market and other issues, Tony appears uncomfortable. He doesn't try to fit in and feign interest in topics that are foreign to him. Nor is he willing to tell mob stories to entertain them; that too would be false, a way of ingratiating himself. Later, Tony reflects that he felt used by them and that he was simply invited for their amusement.

Many leaders today seem as if they're taking on the role of leader rather than allowing their own natural leadership qualities to emerge. While they may be skilled at modeling the "five standard traits" of leaders or exhibiting the "eight characteristics" of the "new" leader, their act wears thin after a while. Sooner or later, people realize when someone isn't allowing her true self to emerge. Being genuine means reacting instead of just acting, and Tony reacts in ways that at times aren't flattering but demonstrate that he is being himself. For instance, at one point Tony becomes upset with Dr. Melfi when she charges him for a missed appointment. He views this action as a sign that she looks at him as nothing more than a money machine and doesn't really care about him as a person. Tony could have played it cool; he could have just pretended that he didn't care she was charging him. Because he was genuinely hurt by her billing him, though, he reacts with righteous indignation. Though his reaction might make him appear cheap or, even worse, vulnerable to her opinion of him, he doesn't care. He's going to be genuine no matter what.

Here's how you can use authenticity, competence, and confidence to add to your charisma:

- Review your actions from the past month for doubt and uncertainty. Use your office calendar to jog your memory; what you're searching for are times when your actions or words betrayed your lack of confidence in yourself and others. Make a list of how you might have exhibited doubt to remind yourself not to turn yourself into the type of leader who appears indecisive and lost.

- Think about what you have to be confident about. Specifically, focus on your competencies. What are you good at? Are you a terrific speaker? Have you always been great at coming up with new ideas at a moment's notice? Do you do a good job at building relationships and networking? To project a confident air, it helps to remind yourself occasionally that you do excel at specific things.

- Create a phony/genuine chart. In other words, on one side of a piece of paper list the common things you do or say that don't reflect who you are. Here are three examples:
  1. Sucking up to your boss
  2. Pretending that the lousy research reports your direct reports give you are "pretty good"
  3. Making excuses to your staff about why you can't go to ball games with them because you have other commitments

On the genuine side, write how you might act more authentically when this situation comes up again. Here are the three genuine responses to the three phony actions listed:

1. Respectfully telling the boss that his "brilliant" new policy to increase accountability is actually a paperwork nightmare that will have his people cursing him until the day they die
2. Confronting direct reports and explaining exactly why their research fails to cut the mustard
3. Go to the ball games if you really feel like going, and if you don't, telling your staff honestly why you don't want to go

Strength and the Perception of Invincibility

In our kinder, gentler world, many leaders have "softened" their images to be more accessible. They have moved away from the strong, silent type to a more touchy-feely persona. In many ways, this is a good trend. Leaders today need to humanize themselves and learn to relate to people better than leaders did in the past. Some executives, though, have carried this trend too far. They appear to lack a backbone. They seem to give in to the slightest bit of pressure from above and fail to support their people when they're having problems. In consensus-driven cultures, especially, the message may be that passionate debate is unacceptable, and leaders embrace this message by not expressing their ideas strongly.

As I'm sure you know, Tony isn't like this. His crew sees him as someone who stands up for himself and his people. He does not let anyone get away with anything, and he does not let anyone walk over him. Even though he doesn't particularly like Ralph, Tony knows that he has to protect Ralph when it appears as though Johnny Sack is after him and beats one of his men for no apparent reason. In addition, when Carmine and Johnny are looking to get a piece of the HUD deal, Tony doesn't automatically cave in to their pressure. Instead, because he doesn't agree that they should get a big piece of the action, he decides to shut down the Esplanade and wait them out until they come up with a more realistic offer. He knows that his organization is more diversified than Carmine's and that he could force their hand. Despite the pressure they put on him, Tony refuses to back down, even though they give him opportunities to compromise without losing face. Part of projecting an image of strength is refusing to compromise even a little bit when you're sure you're right, and in this instance, Tony is certain his position is the right one.

You know a leader is strong when he's emulated by his people. There are many Tony wanna-bes, and Artie, the restaurant owner, is one of them. Artie's hostess's brother is late for payment on the loan Artie made him. At first, Artie tries to be a nice guy, but when that doesn't work, he decides to strong-arm the brother into giving him the money. Before visiting his delinquent customer, Artie does his best Tony impersonation in front of a mirror. He then bursts into the guy's apartment, tries to beat him up, and gets pounded himself. Still, it's a testament to Tony's strength as a leader that Artie wants to be just like him.

In fact, Tony is so charismatically strong as a leader that other people reflexively model their behaviors after him. Even Dr. Melfi, when she's at a restaurant and has had a few drinks, assumes Tony's tough-guy stance. The woman sitting at the next table has been smoking cigarettes and Dr. Melfi has asked her to stop. Dr. Melfi sounds remarkably like Tony when she stops being the polite professional and barks the order to "Put the goddamn cigarette out!" Jackie Jr., too, attempts to emulate Tony's style when he stages a robbery of a high-stakes card game and ends up shooting the dealer and two made men. Like Artie, Jackie Jr. admires Tony's strength but fails when he tries to imitate it. Therein lies a lesson. I'm not suggesting that you should become a swaggering tough guy as a leader. There are many different ways to be strong, and you need to choose the way that fits your personality and position.

Charismatic strength often involves an air of invincibility. Tony seems indestructible in general and more specifically when he survives an attempt on his life; he appears to be so physically strong and forceful that nothing can harm him. Leaders in business seem invincible because they project qualities such as resoluteness and determination in the face of stiff odds. It's not just that these leaders survive internal politics and various downsizings, but that they stick to their positions and policies despite pressures from outside (customers) and inside (bosses, consultants, boards) to get them to change. The phrase "indomitable will" captures what these people are all about. Such strength can be magnetic and inspire followers. People want to be associated with winners.

The danger of being a strong leader is that it can make people overly depend on you. When Christopher gets himself in a jam after hijacking Junior's trucks, he turns to Tony and asks, "What do we do, T?" In the "Pine Barrens" episode when Christopher and Paulie are lost in the words, Paulie frequently calls Tony and ask for instructions. Consciously or not, strong leaders may feel the need to create this overdependence. Wanting Christopher to assume more responsibility within the family, Tony arranges for Christopher to kill the man who "supposedly" killed his father. He knew that this had been hanging over Christopher's head for quite a while and was an unresolved issue. Tony manipulates the events in such a way that Christopher would forever be beholden to him.

If you want to develop the type of leadership strength that inspires others, here are some techniques to use:

- Identify your particular mode of strength. Maybe you're the type who fights long and hard to implement your programs and ideas. Maybe you're strong in the sense that you support your people through thick and thin. Maybe your strength resides in remaining calm and making good decisions in volatile situations. Maybe your strength is in your character; you never kowtow to anyone or attempt to manipulate people to do your bidding. Find your strength and project it as often and in as many ways as possible.

- Don't give in, back down, or renege on a promise. These are the type of actions that cause leaders to be perceived as weak. Bosses who promise direct reports bonuses and then have to rescind their promises because they "couldn't get approval" or "this is a bad time to ask for it" are seen as weak-willed. Similarly, managers who give rousing talks to their people about how they're going to obtain resource X for the group or get Executive Y off their backs and then have to back down from this pledge are also viewed as lily-livered. Just avoiding these weak actions—or at least avoiding them as much as you can—will help foster a perception of strength.

- Be sufficiently confident in your strength that you don't create a race of slaves. In today's business environment, leaders must foster a sense of interdependence in their people. They need to convey the importance of acting independently but also as part of a larger group. Dependent employees will constantly seek your permission and approval, and this dependence will rob them of initiative and creativity. Therefore, don't be so intimidating that people are afraid to make a move without your say-so. Don't be so high-and-mighty that they automatically attempt to please you first and solve the problem second. Give people sufficient freedom to act on their own without fear of reprisals from you if they make a mistake.

Comfort with Power

With leadership comes power, but not all leaders are comfortable with this power or understand how to use it. Some abuse their power by humiliating direct reports or treating vendors with a cavalier disregard. Others are so cowed by it that they never use it at all, pretending they're just like everyone else. In either case, they never benefit from the charisma that comes to leaders comfortable with their power.

Tony is comfortable with his power. Certainly, at times he abuses it, but most of the time, it fits him like a glove. While he needs his power, he doesn't let it dominate him. He respects his own power without fearing it. And he always reminds his people—sometimes in subtle ways—that the power is his. Even when he is with his guys eating a plate of macaroni, he always sits at the head of the table. At a crowded restaurant, the thought of waiting for a table never enters his mind. Tony tailors his use of power to fit the situation. Sometimes, he'll use it to put people in their place. In every interaction with Vin, the "degenerate gambler" police detective, Tony treats him with a barely disguised disdain. In one scene after Vin has given Tony information on Dr. Melfi's movements (Tony was not sure if she might be working for the Feds), Tony is carrying a box of macaroons. Vin asks him what is in the box and requests a cookie. Tony pauses, not immediately giving him one. This simple gesture says a lot. Tony sees him as weak and does not respect weakness. When the FBI comes with a search warrant to his home, Tony retains his powerful demeanor. When one of the agents breaks a bowl he took from the refrigerator, Tony orders him to clean it up.

TONY ON ACCEPTING
LEADERSHIP RESPONSIBILITY

"I'm the one who calls the shots."

Tony also never lingers at a meeting; he speaks his piece and then leaves. He gives you his undivided attention, accomplishes the task but never acts as if his power is so insecure that he must oversee the meeting or that he has to be like everyone else and stay because his power makes him uncomfortable. His quick exits from meetings convey that he has other important matters to attend to, that you may have the luxury of engaging in chitchat but he does not.

Tony is not always subtle about letting others know he's in charge, especially if they seem to forget this fact or disrespect him. For example, he never passed up an opportunity to taunt Junior's driver and consigliere, Mikey Palmice. After a few runins with him, Tony finally beats him up and then uses a staple gun to indelibly imprint the lesson of who's in charge. This is Junior's right-hand man, but Tony doesn't hesitate to put him in his place; Tony is powerful enough that he doesn't fear the consequences.

It's also important to note that Tony doesn't squander his power. He recognizes that sometimes it makes more sense to use influence rather than brute force. It would be easy for Tony to use his clout to undermine Junior. Instead, he recognizes it's wiser to treat Junior as an equal than as someone who is beneath him. To keep peace in the family, therefore, he perpetuates the illusion that Junior is in charge. When Junior wants to tax Hesh, Tony works with Johnny Sack to arrange the sit-down with Junior and Hesh but makes it appear as though Johnny Sack is calling the shots. It saves Hesh money, makes it clear to Johnny who is in charge, and retains Junior as the figurehead. When Hesh and others complain to Tony that Junior isn't spreading around the take, Tony speaks to Junior and remedies the situation. What Tony does not do, however, is tell everyone that he was responsible for achieving this goal. He lets it go unsaid, and the fact that he doesn't have to brag about it testifies to his power.

Finally, Tony radiates the aura of power by dealing only with his equals. When he meets with Teittleman, the Hasidic Jew, Teittleman asks for Tony's help in securing his daughter's divorce, and Tony shows Teittleman respect by asking him to call him by his first name and by being empathetic about his daughter's situation. When Teittleman's son tries to speak to Tony, though, Tony ignores him. Similarly, when Tony goes to Italy to arrange a deal with his "brethren" there, he makes it clear that he will deal only with the "big boss." When he discovers that the big boss is Annalisa—all the men are in jail—he is at first taken aback but soon shows her the respect due an equal.

Here are two ways you can be a powerful leader in the best sense of that word:

1. Analyze your power comfort level by answering the following questions:
   - Do you feel the need to constantly remind people you're in charge?
   - Do you worry that peers will think you're a power-crazed jerk and therefore do everything possible to pretend you're their peer?
   - Do you use your power selectively and strategically; do you wait for the right moment and the right situation to flex your muscles?
   - Can you get people to pay attention to you without raising your voice or doing anything else out of the ordinary?
   - When someone disrespects your position or tries to usurp some of your power, do you make sure he understands he's made a mistake?
2. Create a list of ways you can show people your power without being obvious or obnoxious about it. One example is the way Tony never lingers at meetings. Another example might be communicating only with people on your level when important alliances or deals are being discussed. Another possibility might involve correcting someone who directly or indirectly challenges your authority (rather than letting it slide).

CHARISMA IS IN THE EYE OF THE BEHOLDER

You may view yourself as a charismatic leader but everyone else thinks you're a big blowhard. Or you may be convinced that your quiet, unassuming style is as far from charismatic as possible, but your people feel like you're a dynamic, magnetic leader. You can't just go by personality type to determine if you're charismatic. Tony is very different from John F. Kennedy, who is very different from Oprah Winfrey, who is very different from Woody Allen, who is very different from Tiger Woods. Therefore, don't look in the mirror seeking your charisma. Instead, have other people look at you and provide you with feedback. The following are implied questions to distribute to direct reports, revolving around the four underlying elements of charisma that Tony possesses. Ideally, they'll provide you with honest feedback. Even if they don't, you can use these ideas to reflect on what you need to do to become the type of leader who has presence.

Rate your boss based on a 1–5 scale:

1. My manager goes to bat for our group with regard to raises, promotions, resources, etc.
5	4	3	2	1
All the time		Sometimes		Never

2. My manager acts according to deeply held beliefs and values about how business should be conducted.
5	4	3	2	1
All the time		Sometimes		Never

3. My manager speaks and acts authentically; what you see is what you get.
5	4	3	2	1
All the time		Sometimes		Never

4. My manager always seems to know exactly what she's doing.
5	4	3	2	1
All the time		Sometimes		Never

5. My manager exhibits great confidence in his programs and policies.

5	4	3	2	1
All the time		Sometimes		Never

6. My manager is seen as a player in this organization.

5	4	3	2	1
All the time		Sometimes		Never

7. My manager is comfortable with power, rarely using it unnecessarily or arbitrarily.

5	4	3	2	1
All the time		Sometimes		Never

8. My manager seems like she couldn't possibly fail.

5	4	3	2	1
All the time		Sometimes		Never

Maybe you're never going to have Tony's electricity, but you can certainly increase the wattage with which you burn. As you receive the responses to these statements or reflect on how people might respond, make your goal to move "one-up" in four of the eight categories. In other words, you just need to move from *never* to *sometimes* or *sometimes* to *all the time* relative to four of the numbered responses. This may seem like a modest gain in charisma on paper, but in real work life, people will notice.

> ### TONY'S CHARISMA AHA!
> Enter a room like it's your own kitchen instead of some hoity-toity mansion where you're afraid of using the wrong fork.

3

WHO'S THE BOSS

A Simple, Clear, and Adaptive Structure

Some leaders today become lost in their companies' "creative" and overly complex organizational structures. As they focus on innovation and work processes, they may lose some degree of effectiveness.

Tony would have problems as a leader in a matrixed organization where consensus decision making was prized and unilateral decision making was discouraged. As a leader who prizes execution above all else, Tony favors a pragmatic structure that emphasizes informal yet clear reporting relationships. No fancy matrix structures or multiple reporting relationships for him. Roles are clear. Areas of responsibility and accountability are precisely laid out. Direct reports are not allowed to "play out of position" within this structure unless they are trying to make a move on the boss or on a territory—a dangerous and unusual gambit.

At first glance, it may appear that Tony runs a typical and slightly outdated command-and-control structure. Tony's organization chart certainly mirrors the larger mob hierarchical structure, employing a militaristic model, as illustrated on page 42.

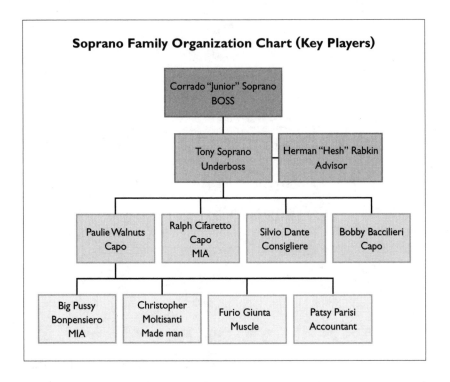

Tony, however, recognizes the need for a fluid structure in a volatile environment and provides his crew with a remarkable amount of leeway, especially in such a buttoned-up organization. Every business leader can learn a lot from the way Tony works effectively and innovatively within a seemingly rigid structure. Let's look at what this structure is all about and how Tony makes the most out of it.

POSITIVES AND NEGATIVES OF THE DEADLY EFFICIENT ORGANIZATION

In the mob model, captains generally oversee several crews headed up by soldiers, and unquestioning obedience is the operating principle. Christopher, for instance, is a soldier. Two of his associates, Sean and Matt, started out committing small burglaries, but when they disobeyed—they tried to gun down Christopher as a favor to Richie—they did not receive the type of warning a direct report might receive for a similar act of disrespect. Instead, they received immediate termination notices. They did not obtain support from Richie or anyone else. Clearly, they had overstepped their authority based on the mob's structure, and in a hierarchy where reporting relationships are sacred, they committed a terrible sin.

It's understandable how the mob benefits from this structure. Without rigid reporting relationships and an emphasis on obedience, chaos might erupt. People might stage internal coups or form alliances with other families that could destroy the organization. Bosses need to keep a tight rein on their people to ensure they don't get any bright ideas and start acting as free agents.

While Tony needs to work within this structure, he has made adjustments that allow him to be more innovative than most mob bosses. As you can see from the chart on page 44, Tony has blurred certain lines that normally are crystal clear so that there is overlapping responsibility for various businesses.

Tony's intense pragmatism informs this structure. He is not going to push decision making down to its lowest level because he doesn't trust neophytes or guys who are all brawn and no brains. Nor is he going to encourage his people to network without his direction and supervision, aware that they could just as easily form alliances against him as for him. Though Tony's ego is healthy, he has more practical reasons for giving himself so much power. He knows that in the mob culture, a boss without power is a boss who will never receive respect. Following are the underlying assumptions of Tony's structure:

- Following the chain of command is good and keeps things orderly.
- These guys are crooks and need rules to keep them together.

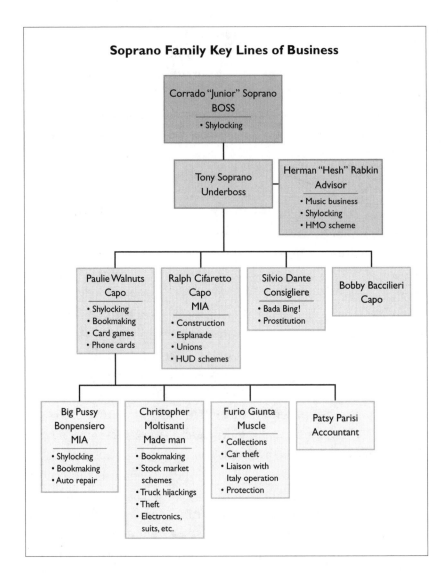

Soprano Family Key Lines of Business

Corrado "Junior" Soprano
BOSS
• Shylocking

Tony Soprano
Underboss

Herman "Hesh" Rabkin
Advisor
• Music business
• Shylocking
• HMO scheme

Paulie Walnuts
Capo
• Shylocking
• Bookmaking
• Card games
• Phone cards

Ralph Cifaretto
Capo
MIA
• Construction
• Esplanade
• Unions
• HUD schemes

Silvio Dante
Consigliere
• Bada Bing!
• Prostitution

Bobby Baccilieri
Capo

Big Pussy
Bonpensiero
MIA
• Shylocking
• Bookmaking
• Auto repair

Christopher
Moltisanti
Made man
• Bookmaking
• Stock market
  schemes
• Truck hijackings
• Theft
• Electronics,
  suits, etc.

Furio Giunta
Muscle
• Collections
• Car theft
• Liaison with
  Italy operation
• Protection

Patsy Parisi
Accountant

- Following orders is okay; it's the way things are done; no one objects to this.
- The boss has the final word. You can give him all your input and disagree, but he has the last word. Once a decision is reached, it is executed without further argument or disagreement. Everyone stands behind the decision.

- You respect the boss. The boss is the boss because he is the right man for the job. He has proven himself. He knows what he is doing. The other families respect him.
- You trust the people at the top; they earned their stripes.
- Your loyalty is to the family and to the person above you. The family will take care of you, especially if you are in need.

Reading these assumptions, you may want to tell Tony to get out of the dark ages and get with contemporary organization design. At the very least, you may think that none of his assumptions apply to your leadership role. You probably responded to all the ideas about loyalty to the family and following orders as irrelevant to what you're trying to accomplish today. Who is loyal to organizations in these times? Who follows orders, especially among the growing, youthful management information systems (MIS) segment of the employee population?

TONY ON THE FUNCTION OF DIRECT REPORTS FROM A LEADERSHIP PERSPECTIVE

"Your job is to make my job easier."

If you don't take these assumptions 100 percent literally, though, you might find some figurative truth in Tony's structural imperatives. Consider his premise that "these guys are crooks and need rules to keep them together." I'm assuming your people aren't crooks, but they may be headstrong, immature, and overly willing to take risks. Thus, they need some rules—some well-defined parameters—by which to operate effectively.

To see how Tony's structural principles may apply to the 21st-century leader, let's imagine what might happen if Tony decided to hire a management consultant to provide him with an alternative perspective on the way he's organized his crew. This consultant is relatively young and very much in favor of all the hot concepts, and Tony calls him in to discuss his view of Tony's group. Here is how their conversation might go:

> **Management consultant:** Tony, the pyramid is out. Haven't you heard that we want to push decision making down and empower people?
>
> **Tony:** Hey, I push it as far down as I can. My captains run their own shows. As long as they bring in the money. That's all that matters. They bring in their take 'cause they don't want me up their can. They decide how they do it and by what means they'll do it. I expect that they do that with their crews and down the line. I don't want to ride anybody and I don't want my guys to ride anybody. No one wants to work that way. The associates under the soldiers, well that's another story. We don't give them much rope. These guys are green. They have to prove that they can take orders and they have to prove that they can be trusted.
>
> **Management consultant:** With such a hierarchical structure, you cannot possibly benefit by getting ideas from those lower in the organization—those closest to the work. Your captains are so removed from the day-to-day operations.
>
> **Tony:** You saying that my captains don't know what's going on with their crews? I expect my captains to be on top of their soldiers and I expect my soldiers to be on top of their associates—that's how it works. Everybody knows what's going on below them at the levels they need to know it. This also is not a dictatorship but it's also not a democracy, either. The soldiers have their say with the capos and my capos have their say with me. Everybody speaks his mind but the boss always has the last word. Once we make a decision, it is executed with no one speaking in opposition.

Management consultant: What other benefits do you find with this structure?

Tony: It's fast and efficient. If there's a problem, someone calls me and we take care of it. If it's something that affects all of us, we get together and talk about it. Problems in any part of the business are either taken care of at the source by the capos or the soldiers or the problems filter up to me and we resolve 'em. Me and my captains are tight. We are loyal to the family, we trust each other with our lives. We tell each other everything. I lay it all on the line and I expect them to do the same. If there's an issue with trust, well then I have to deal with it.

Management consultant: Who heads up new business?

Tony (*Laughs*): Everybody is responsible for new business. I want all my guys to be thinking up new scams, looking at who we can strong-arm into needing protection, targeting the degenerate gamblers who's business is ripe for the taking, more "no-show" construction jobs. Well, you get the picture. Anyone who has a new idea for a scheme presents the idea to his boss and gets a go-no-go decision. If the scheme involves a large crew, an outlay of a lot of money, or associates outside our family, the capos may need to get together and discuss it. It most situations, the head of the crew can make the call.

Management consultant: One of the things I've observed with hierarchical organizations is that it is difficult to be exposed to the talent below you.

Tony: Again, I rely on my capos to spot the guys who show some promise. They test them, throw them some line to see how they do. They will sometimes let me know if there is someone I should see. We can give 'em a shot with a shakedown, fetching drinks at the executive card game. If he is worth it, I'll get a look.

Management consultant: With everything having to go through the chain of command, what happens if I have a beef with my boss? Who do I go to?

Tony: You got a legitimate beef, you can call a sit-down. You get heard and a decision is made. But you gotta follow whatever decision is made. These are the rules.

Management consultant: I know that Paulie has some gambling business and so does Sil; I am not sure how efficient it is to have gambling and loan-sharking operations under more than one person.

Tony: Paulie's got his bookies that have been with him for years. They will do business only with him. Paulie also has this handful of high rollers that he lets lose so much and then he stops them. Paulie always knows how much they can lose and how many points they can actually afford at one time. I don't know how he does it but he never misses. If I gave these to Sil, well they might get so far behind, that we'd have to kill them. What good is that? Lastly, there's Hesh, he's got so much money for loan-sharking and he's such a pussycat at first with his circle, that as long as he gives us our due, we all eat.

You also gotta remember that what an individual may be responsible for may have more to do with his area of expertise, what was passed down to him by his family, and what contacts he has that can be leveraged versus what neat box he fits into.

I can also easily shift around responsibilities. I don't like to do it that often . . . unless it's necessary. If there's a question of trust or we think a guy might have flipped, well, then we have to take some precautions.

Management consultant: A real disadvantage to your structure is that there is no crossover or sharing of guys between the crews.

Tony (*Looks at him with a steely glare*): And who and how do you think pulled off that hit on the Colombians?

Or the HUD deal? Need I say more? We get the best guys for whatever job we need to pull off—no matter who's crew they are in. We all share in the money. We're very flexible and can adapt and shift as we need to.

Management consultant: You make it sound like they are all one big happy family. There's no fighting or rivalry?

Tony: Basically, we all do get along—some better than others. Rivalry, competition, I guess so. That's normal. Everyone wants to be the big earner, that's part of how you get your stripes. Everybody knows who's earning and who's behind. As long as it's healthy though, it's good for business. The more deals we can make, the more everybody earns. Sabotaging or stealing from another crew or poaching on another's territory, it's against the rules. You'll pay big time.

Management consultant: Have you ever thought about a different type of structure like a council where decisions are made by a group?

Tony: Yeah, we talked about it once. I remember we were eating lobsters. It was right after Jackie died. We knew there was the need for a leader but no one wanted to step up. No one really wanted the headaches, the Feds up your wazoo, so one of the guys suggested we run the family like a council, but then we said that the old guys set it up like a paramilitary organization. You need a boss. It works. Sometimes the young guys might not like it as much. Christopher was not real happy when I brought Furio in without "consulting" him. I remember he smarted off and said, "I didn't get the memo [about Furio]." I smarted right back with, "Would you have read it if you would've gotten one?" I don't consult them on everything. That's the way it is.

Management consultant: After Jackie died, there was some vying for power between you and Junior. Did you ever think about trying out some type of coleadership arrangement between the two of you?

Tony: You gotta be nuts. Listen, I love the man. He's my uncle, but coleadership, no way. We're as different as night and day. His guys are loyal to him and my guys to me. If we disagreed over something, we'd probably end up killing each other. Maybe coleaders works if you're Ben and Jerry and running an ice-cream company, but not in our line of work. People need one boss.

A SIMPLE STRUCTURE FOR COMPLEX TIMES

Think about your company and the particular group you're part of. What's the worst thing about the way it's set up? I've asked this question of different executives in different companies, and here are some of their responses:

- It takes forever to turn an idea into a program.
- The system is set up so that we can't move on anything until we reach consensus, and consensus often means compromised ideas. Plus, it slows things down.
- Responsibility is divided creatively but unclearly; we have a lot of synergy but not much follow-through.
- We're supposed to have knowledge exchanges, but there's no real incentive for people to share their ideas with other groups.
- We have so many teams working on so many different projects that it's tough to coordinate everyone's efforts.
- When market conditions change, we're not set up to change with them. We're such a big, complex company that we lack flexibility.
- Our flattened structure lets us move quickly, but the way it turns out, we have ten different groups moving quickly in ten different directions.

Take a moment and assess whether your structure is as adaptable, simple, and clear as the Soprano family organization. To help you with your assessment, I've created the ABC Quiz, which asks you to assume that your company is in a business similar to that of the Soprano family. If Tony were to take this quiz, he'd pass with flying colors. Most business leaders in most organizations would fail; see how you and your organization fare.

ABC Quiz

1. If you were trying to schedule a "hit" on one of your competitors, how fast could you assemble and free the right team of people?

   a. Overnight
   b. A week
   c. A month

2. If your top team and Tony's top team (Paulie, Sil, and Christopher) were in a competition to see which team was more cohesive and trustworthy, how would your team do?

   a. We're ready to take 'em on (remember, Paulie does talk to Johnny Sack every so often).
   b. We'd probably come in third . . . that is assuming there would be another team. Team, what team?
   c. We'd get creamed.

3. You and your team see an opportunity to corner the market on fenced plasma TVs and you come up with a great strategy. Other factions of your organization, however, raise objections to your strategy once they realize you're going ahead with it. You don't think these objections are valid, but their strenuous objections give you pause. Would you:

   a. Keep going? They had their chance to voice their concerns during the planning phase.
   b. Understand their concerns but continue moving forward?
   c. Stop the presses!? Regroup and revisit the strategy.

4. Your team recently spent a full day with the Supply Chain "probabilities" team (your bookies) clarifying roles, responsibilities, and decision rights. Who does what is all mapped out. Two weeks later, one of the bookies "plays out of position," doing a major piece of work that one of your team members was supposed to do. You:

   a. Call the head bookie immediately and meet and clarify roles and responsibilities.
   b. Call the bookie who played out of position and get in his face about his mistake.
   c. Let it go. You don't want to deal with the crazy bookie and figure it won't happen again.

5. One of your direct reports who also has a dotted-line reporting relationship to one of your peers comes to you because your peer has threatened to whack him if he continues to prioritize the assignments you give him. You:

   a. Call a sit-down with your peer and your direct report to resolve the issues, but make it clear that the way things are structured, you have the last word on this subject.
   b. Tell your direct report to suck up to your peer but continue to prioritize the assignments you give him.
   c. Do nothing. It will sort itself out.

6. You believe you need to hire someone externally who has expertise in an area your team is lacking experience in—you're looking for a safecracker who is skilled at digital combinations. Your team is upset—they think they can handle this assignment internally—and communicate they're against the hire. You:

   a. Hire the person. It's your decision.
   b. Put off the decision for a while. Take some time to educate your team on the intricacies of cracking a digital combination safe and wait to hire the person until they change their mind.
   c. Don't hire the person. You don't want to upset things right now.

7. You issue a directive informing everyone that from this moment forward, all interactions with buyers of stolen goods, prostitution and gambling customers, and partners in all scams and schemes must be

summarized in a report and submitted within one day. Your people would:

a. Immediately do what you ask without questions or reservations.
b. Do what you ask but drag their feet a bit.
c. Question your directive and passively resist doing it.

8. One of your direct reports tells you he's quitting the business to find less risky work. You are:

a. Not surprised because your extensive contacts in your industry told you when he started interviewing for other jobs.
b. A little surprised but had a sense that he was unhappy.
c. Shocked. You didn't see it coming.

9. You hear a rumor that one of your best customers is going to "flip" to your competitor. Where did you hear this rumor?

a. From your right-hand man, who heard it from his right-hand man; your network always communicates this type of customer information quickly and accurately.
b. From your wife, who happened to overhear it over lunch.
c. Rumor, what rumor?

10. You've never wanted to get into the casino business because it appears to invite too much federal scrutiny, but you meet a politician who you trust and who has the clout to minimize that scrutiny. You:

a. Immediately change your strategic plan and get into the casino business.
b. Form a committee to study the feasibility of entering the casino business.
c. Adhere to your current strategy and avoid the casino business because you're afraid to try something that had a lot of risk attached to it in the past.

Scoring:

More than eight a's: Tony will make you his right-hand man.

Half a's and half b's: Junior needs a flunky.

Mostly c's: You can be the assistant manager of a strip club.

THE ADVANTAGES OF THE SOPRANO STRUCTURE

Though the previous quiz was clearly tongue in cheek, it suggests why Tony's group functions so effectively. As I indicated earlier, Tony's superior business strategy and the way he builds trust and loyalty contribute to his team's effectiveness. Clarity, simplicity, and adaptability are the most obvious elements of his structure, but three other aspects of the Soprano organization also contribute to its ability to achieve goals and deliver results. Let's look at all five individually and how you can capitalize on them:

1. Clarity and simplicity
2. Adaptability
3. Free-flowing communication
4. A process to resolve conflict
5. Rituals

Clarity and Simplicity

Many leaders long for the days when they knew exactly who in their organization was responsible for what, when teams weren't working on parallel tracks, and when they didn't have to peruse a phonebook-thick organization manual to figure out what they could and couldn't do. Tony's organization, therefore, represents a return to the days of clarity and simplicity. It also largely avoids the problem with the traditional approach: being too simple to deal effectively with all the gray issues that arise.

As you watch Tony and his people make money, you marvel at the clarity of their work processes. Someone is always unambiguously in charge. Everyone knows who to go to for help or for a decision. The captain and his crew know their targets and move toward them quickly and efficiently. This is in contrast to many organizations where the goals or expected output aren't clear. I know one organization that spent months developing ten key-performance indicators, but the measures of those indicators were so complex that no one could follow them. The company ended up revising that list the next year, but at the end of that year when it was time to give out the bonuses attached to those indicators and measures, people began disagreeing with the measures and the data associated with them.

Tony's structure also addresses the issue of unclear accountabilities. In organizations with complex or matrixed structures, people find places to hide or scapegoats when things don't get done. Multiple reporting relationships or teams with shared responsibilities make it difficult to discover who is in charge and who can make a decision. While matrix organizations are very useful in certain ways, they also require clarifying and reclarifying roles, accountabilities, and decision-making authority. They can muddy the decision-making waters in conflict-averse cultures, for no one wants to acknowledge that one individual has more power than the other. As a result, decision-making power is shared, and this results in coleadership situations, the type that Tony despises (as seen, for example, when it was suggested he share power with Junior).

Accountability is much clearer in Tony's group. Profound consequences exist when you fail to do what you're supposed to do or you do something that is taboo. While I'm not suggesting that employees be shot in the head for failing to complete an assignment, a small but healthy amount of fear is a strong motivator. Today, in some organizations, people often aren't particularly afraid of being fired for it takes a significant amount of documentation to terminate someone. Raises and promotions tend to be smaller these days, so fear of not getting a big bonus isn't the motivator it once was. Nonetheless, in the right system, bosses can set specific consequences tied to accountability that cause direct reports to "respect" their responsibilities. By clarifying roles and establishing negative sanctions for playing out of position or being a lone wolf, leaders can increase the odds that people will do what they're supposed to do. As long as there's no ambiguity about these consequences—the organization doesn't promote great individual contributors who refuse to play on teams, for instance—then people will respond positively.

Adaptability

Organizations have made efforts to become more flexible in recent years, relying on everything from flatter structures to processes that allow certain individuals and teams to circumvent the bureaucracy to make fast decisions. Too often, though, these innovations provide adaptability in name only. Often there is the sense that company flexibility-facilitating programs are mere window dressing; that management doesn't want its people to veer away from traditional approaches without going through a lengthy approval process. As a result, most people in companies don't take advantage of opportunities to adapt.

At first glance, Tony's structure doesn't seem to encourage flexible attitudes or behaviors. His top-down structure tends to put people in boxes, defining their roles and responsibilities so clearly that they're not allowed to adapt as situations dictate for fear of crossing boundaries. Tony, however, gives his people a significant amount of freedom to violate these boundaries if it will help them solve problems and, above all else, make more money. In effect, he sets up a paradoxical system in which people are constrained by the structure but encouraged to violate it if common sense tells them they should. Of course, Tony's guys better be able to justify their violations or they'll pay a price. His people, though, know the rules and that Tony's system accommodates rule violations if they're warranted.

In a way, this represents the best of both worlds. The explicit structure provides clarity of roles and responsibilities, but the implicit freedom from roles and responsibilities—if such freedom can be justified—offers opportunities to adjust to changing circumstances. Perhaps more companies should adopt this paradoxical structure if they want to achieve "accountable flexibility." Of course, Tony has an advantage because he makes sure everyone in his organization understands and respects goals and boundaries. Tony gives people the freedom to be flexible because he has made sure they know what they can and cannot do.

TONY ON INCULCATING RULES INTO THE CULTURE

"I don't make the rules.
They've always been there."

Free-Flowing Communication

Though I'll talk more about communication in Chapter 6, I'd like to emphasize how Tony's structure often creates a good flow of information both up and down the organization chart. Tony has made sure all his people understand the psychology of this structure. In other words, they all recognize that they're linked together like climbers on a mountain, and that if one falls off, they all fall off. Even the lowliest associate generally feels connected to his peers, his boss, and the family as a whole. Tony's behavior models how he values these connections. Even though Junior is a pain, Tony bends over backwards to accommodate him. Even though he knows Richie is psychotic, he treats him fairly until Richie pushes Tony too far. Because Tony's attitude and actions toward everyone are based on their positions within the overall structure, that structure garners respect.

As a result, information and ideas generally flow freely. People feel too connected to other people in the family to hide important information, though there are some exceptions—Paulie recently has become disgruntled and is more reticent around Tony than he had been. Still, there's a remarkable openness, not only in terms of sharing good news but sharing bad news as well.

It's why season in and season out, Tony's crew seems to prosper when others do not.

TONY ON THE NEED
FOR OPENNESS AND HONESTY

"Why don't we put our cards on the table."

If you're like most executives, you occasionally become frustrated because knowledge becomes "stuck" in various corporate corners. An individual believes he'll be better off if he hoards ideas, sharing them only when he feels such sharing will benefit him the most. Members of a team keep their research and discoveries to themselves because they fear a competing team will capitalize on their hard work and come up with a solution before they do. Or a particular department absolutely refuses to communicate consistently and openly with another department based on years of mutual antipathy. Unfortunately, information sharing is not part of the culture or the individual mind-set in most organizations.

While Tony's structure doesn't eliminate the tension between various factions or individual selfishness, it does help minimize it. Most of the time, Tony's people recognize that they're better off communicating important information quickly to the individual below or above them. They may not always like sharing, but Tony makes sure they know that they'll like the alternative even less.

A Process to Resolve Conflict

When a significant problem between individuals or groups crops up in organizations, no one knows quite what to do. Typically, a series of meetings is held to resolve the problem; leaders meet with the individuals involved separately and together. Sometimes, though, leaders do nothing, hoping that the problem will disappear on its own. In other instances, people are transferred to other groups or a leader lays down the law and insists all the bickering stop immediately. Rarely, though, is there a systematic process in place to resolve conflict that everyone understands and accepts.

Tony possesses such a process, and it is a structural element of his organization. This process must have been born out of necessity. When you're dealing with violent criminals and lack a dispute resolution process, the likely outcome is that disputes will be resolved with blood. To avoid this outcome, Tony's group embraces the sit-down process, the mechanics of which follow.

MECHANICS OF A SIT-DOWN

Ground rules

- A sit-down can be requested by anyone in the organization.
- It is facilitated by a trusted third party (consigliere, underboss, etc.) and sometimes the overall boss.
- The decision by the third party is binding and must be executed.

Process

- The trigger is that an individual requests a sit-down.
- The sit-down is arranged by the previously agreed on/appointed third party.
- The third party may do some fact-finding prior to the sit-down. This would involve talking with both sides and/or those directly involved in the situation.
- The individual who requested the sit-down brings his boss as does the person who the dispute is with.
- Both sides lay out facts. The third party attempts to facilitate a resolution with clear agreements and next steps. If no resolution can be reached, the process moves up the chain of command. The boss of the two parties would facilitate this round. If there were no resolution, a third sit-down would be facilitated by the next level of management and so on.

The best and most humorous example of the process was when Johnny Sack hears from Paulie that Ralph has made a joke about Johnny's wife's weight at a dinner. In the mob world, one of the key rules is that you don't disrespect a man's wife, daughter, or mother. If you disrespect the woman, you disrespect the man. Johnny first takes out his anger by beating up one of Ralph's guys. When Tony finds out, he urges Ralph to placate but not apologize to Johnny; apologizing would be an admission of guilt. When this strategy backfires, Johnny goes to Carmine to request a hit on Ralph. Carmine basically says that he will tax Ralph but that Ralph is too big of an earner to be taken out. Still seeking retribution, Johnny requests a sit-down under the guise of sorting through the no-show arrangements for the Esplanade contracts. At the sit-down are Ralph, Tony, Johnny, and Carmine. Johnny ends up walking out. The process then escalates to the next level, and a meeting is held without Ralph but with Tony (Ralph's boss), Junior, Johnny, Carmine (Johnny's boss), and Sil as a third-party mediator. In this instance, Carmine has the last word and tells Johnny to let it go. They go back and forth on this issue until Johnny agrees to drop it.

Admittedly, a certain amount of acrimony and vacillation marked this process. Yet it allowed both parties to vent their emotions, to feel like something was being done, and to move toward a resolution of the conflict. Too often, either people in organizations are prohibited from expressing their strong feelings or a boss decides about the conflict unilaterally. Psychologically, this is tremendously unsatisfying. Johnny might not have been happy that he couldn't kill Ralph, but at least he felt as if his point had been heard and his feelings acknowledged.

The decision reached in the sit-down is binding and must be carried out, and this widely understood fact causes people to take sit-downs seriously. While some companies use conflict-resolution processes, few people take these approaches seriously because their decisions aren't binding. Not only are sit-down decisions binding, but once a decision is reached, it is not to be discussed or revisited again. It also is an astonishingly democratic and versatile method of resolving conflict. Anyone can call a sit-down, which can be used for everything, from clarifying new business limits to establishing territorial boundaries.

Many organizations lack a process for resolving conflict. In some instances, conflict is resolved by a manager stepping in. Because this is an ad hoc approach, it often carries little weight with employees. In other instances, conflicts are allowed to spiral out of control before anyone does anything. Angry memos, e-mails, and voice mails are exchanged, gossip about the conflict rages, facts are misconstrued, and feelings are hurt before a manager finally steps in. Tony Soprano usually calls for a sit-down before conflicts reach the crisis stage and a significant amount of damage has already been done.

XYZ, a global organization, removed marketing and manufacturing functions from the control of the general manager in each country to achieve economies of scale. They centralized these functions into shared service centers. Invariably, conflicts arose because general managers no longer had control over their resources and face-to-face interactions were infrequent (because of the geographical distance between general managers and service centers). Even worse, this company had a "gentlemanly" culture in which open conflict—and its resolution—were frowned on. People were encouraged to work toward consensus, and airing grievances and arguing loudly were discouraged. As a result, the conflicts involving this shift to the service centers went underground. General managers felt as if they were losing control of their resources and that the resources weren't being allocated properly, but general managers ended up voicing only mild protests to the service center managers. They didn't want to rock the boat, and this created marketing and manufacturing inefficiencies.

XYZ could have used a sit-down process to bring underground conflicts to the surface to resolve them. If you're interested in integrating such a process into your company, here is what you need to do.

DEVELOPING YOUR SIT-DOWN AS A MANAGEMENT PROCESS

Step 1

Decide on how the sit-down will be positioned. Is it to resolve any type of conflict or dispute or just for a specific type of conflict? Who can take advantage of the process? What are your ground rules?

Step 2

Decide what will trigger implementing a sit-down. Who do you tell that you want to have a sit-down? What needs to be done to proceed?

Step 3

Decide who your third-party facilitators will be and how you'll do the fact-finding prior to the sit-down. You may want to determine the questions that you'll ask beforehand.

Step 4

Decide the consequences for not adhering to agreements reached at the sit-down. Be sure everyone, including those at the top, adheres and does not overturn agreements reached.

Step 5

Provide training in facilitation skills or third-party mediation.

Step 6

Communicate the process to those who will be affected.

Rituals

Integral to the structure of Tony's organization are its rituals. Many companies today have dispensed with the extracurricular ceremonies and activities that bind people together. Company picnics, holiday parties, honors (such as "salesperson of the week"), birthday celebrations, and other nonwork aspects of a company's culture often are eliminated. In some instances, these activities are eliminated because of cost concerns, while in others, organizations merge and long-standing rituals no longer seem relevant. And some companies find these activities a waste of time or hokey remnants of the past.

Unfortunately, when organizations excise these rituals they also remove some of the emotional glue that binds people together. Companies become sterile places to work when all they promote is work. The tangential, nonwork traditions are often central to why people stay at organizations; things such as parties and picnics humanize bosses; they allow employees and sometimes their families to get to know each other; they give everyone a chance to play together rather than just work together. All this builds relationships and indirectly benefits a company's ability to retain and attract people; it also fosters better communication.

Tony and his crew share a common language, assumptions, and philosophy. Some may argue that this is because of their ethnic background as well as the fact that they are all men. While this may be true to some extent, the main thing that binds them together are their rituals—rituals that are integrated into the work routine and are crucial parts of belonging to the organization. The Soprano family's rituals include:

- Celebrations when you get your stripes
- Having your boss be the godfather of your child
- Parties at the Bada Bing! when you get out of prison
- Paying homage (passing the envelope or whatever fell off the truck) at funerals, graduations, birthdays
- The annual holiday party for the children
- Sunday dinners at Tony's

Corporate rituals are for all levels of employees and run the gamut, from annual retreats for executives and their families to golf outings to charitable functions sponsored by the company. One organization's ritual was an afternoon softball game scheduled every Friday throughout the summer. This was a highly competitive company that embraced a "Work hard, play hard" philosophy. This ritual allowed people to blow off steam, to toast accomplishments with beer after the game, and to see hard-charging leaders having fun and making fun of themselves when they muffed a fly ball. Another company hosted an annual meeting that involved an elaborate awards ceremony to honor top performers. This company had a warm, relationship-focused culture, which the ceremony served to reinforce. After each award was made, the ceremony stopped and everyone flocked toward the award-winner, giving him or her hugs and kisses and generally treating the winner like he or she had just hit a home run in the bottom of the ninth inning.

Tony respects the traditions of his family and he joins them seamlessly to the business. Just as importantly, he takes the time to ensure that these rituals are carried out effectively. Take a moment and see if your attitudes and actions regarding rituals are up to Tony's standards.

Do you know your company's rituals? Does the company hold any annual parties or outings and, if so, what makes them special and unique to your company; are there charitable events that your company sponsors and that require employee participation; are there annual retreats for executives or other people in the company?

What do you do to facilitate and honor these rituals? Do you host celebrations for your people when they achieve a goal or finish important projects; do you encourage people to participate in company rituals and do you participate?

Can you think of new activities or ceremonies that you might implement if your company is ritual-deficient? Have you ever invited your group to a barbeque or a poker game; have you ever taken your people to the ballpark or racetrack; do you ever propose activities that would allow people to relate to each other in nonwork settings?

STRUCTURING YOUR OWN TEAM, DEPARTMENT, OR ORGANIZATION

The suggestions for these five structural areas are as implementable for CEOs as they are for small teams. Whether your goal is to restructure the entire organization or just tinker with the way your small group operates, you can apply Tony-inspired ideas on the scale that's appropriate for you. It may be that all you can reasonably do at the moment is start establishing some basic rituals for your group, which is terrific. It's also possible that you have the opportunity to use a number of these concepts—you have a great need for a sit-down conflict resolution approach as well as for facilitating more open communication among your people.

Whatever you choose to do, I trust that Tony's way of dealing with structural issues will help you rethink your own attitudes about group operations. At the very least, they should prompt you to rethink some basic assumptions about and consider some alternatives to traditional structures. Or, as Tony might put it:

TONY'S STRUCTURAL AHA!
Don't get too fancy with the way you organize things and make sure your structure is as flexible as a Bada Bing! dancer's muscles.

4

COACHING THE POOBAHS AND THE GOUMBAS

In recent years, coaching has become an increasingly important leadership skill. For many leaders, however, this isn't a natural skill. They may be great at giving orders but not so great at the more subtle art of coaxing and influencing, of offering advice and sharing their wisdom to achieve group goals and further professional development. For this reason, thousands of training programs have sprung up in recent years to help business executives build coaching skills. The programs run the gamut from the three- to ten-step coaching process to emulating the Zen-like qualities of Lakers coach Phil Jackson. While these training programs are usually effective, they sometimes make things more complex than they need to be. If you ask employees what they want in a coach, they'll tell you they want someone who:

- Cares
- Listens and wants to hear what they have to say

- Gives them feedback and let's them know where they stand and what's expected of them
- Lets them know what they need to do to grow and get promoted
- Lets them do their job but gives them help when they need it

Tony Soprano does all these things. He doesn't always do them perfectly—he can be short-tempered with his people and overly relies on fear as a motivational technique—but he is adept at coaching simply, compassionately, and effectively. He does so by:

- Offering straight talk to his guys—they know immediately when they've messed up
- Giving specific feedback about performance expectations and redirecting performance when necessary
- Clarifying what it takes to get ahead

Let's examine each of Tony's coaching strengths and how you can take advantage of them.

Straight Talk

Leaders sometimes fail to say what they really mean, but Tony doesn't mince words. When his people are going offtrack and he wants to get them back on course, he's brilliant at letting them have it with both barrels—in the figurative sense most of the time. Remarkably, Tony isn't heavy-handed when he talks straight to his people, in large part because of his superb timing and great specificity.

TONY ON TELLING IT LIKE IT IS

"I hate the way you fuckin' make me ride you."

In one scene, Tony and Christopher are in Christopher's car, and Tony is aware that Christopher has been experiencing an identity crisis of sorts. A current federal investigation has resulted in media stories in which other members of the crew are mentioned, but Christopher's name has not been included. He is concerned that he is not achieving his career goals and as a result of his fears, he has been acting out. Tony calls him on his behavior, telling him, "We've been under a microscope and I gotta hear on the street that you shot some fuckin' civilian in the foot because you had to wait for buns." Christopher tries to make an excuse, but Tony tells him to shut up. Tony then goes on to say that "Georgie (an associate in Christopher's crew) has vomit on his shirt . . . because you were digging up some body that you clipped three months ago." Christopher again tries to make an excuse and Tony tells him to shut up. Tony finishes with, "People do that shit because they want to get caught . . . I've seen it before . . . it's cowboyitus . . . you want to be a big bad boy."

Perhaps you think Tony was being overly harsh as a coach? Obviously, using obscenities and telling direct reports to shut up aren't coaching techniques I'd recommend (at least in most circumstances). Remember, though, that Tony is coaching in a different context than you or me, and he's simply relying on the language of his culture. Try and look past this and recognize why his coaching was so effective in this instance. He was not using a five-step model to deliver feedback to Christopher. Tony recognized the importance of getting through to Christopher quickly and clearly, aware of the danger of letting Christopher's issues simmer. It took Tony no more than three sentences to drive home his point. Tony also spoke in specifics; his graphic language and referencing key incidents ensured that Christopher grasped that these were the facts and there was no denying them. Though Tony's refusal to listen to excuses violates empathic listening rules, it was a necessary violation. Christopher understood that he had made a mistake, and Tony wanted to hold Christopher accountable for this error. The situation was cut-and-dried, and Tony didn't want Christopher to think that he could somehow weasel his way out of the mistake. As a coach, Tony wanted to impress Christopher that his behavior was unacceptable, and the best way to demonstrate this fact was through direct, unambiguous language.

Performance Expectations

Good coaching is also about creating and communicating clear performance standards and performance expectations. I have often worked with teams, and if you ask five team members what the performance standards are, you receive five different answers. Many times, leaders fail to be explicit about what they expect from the team. In some instances, they assume (falsely) that the team knows what's expected of them. In other situations, they are deliberately vague, fearful that if they make their expectations known, people will feel intimidated or fail to put in the time and energy to exceed these expectations. Whatever the reason, leaders fall short as coaches when their people don't know what's expected of them or harbor false expectations.

Tony makes sure his people know what's required of them, and his lieutenants in turn insist their people also are clear about what's needed from them. There's a trickle-down effect to clear expectations: When the person at the top insists on clarity, the next rank of managers also tends to set clear expectations. Paulie, for instance, lets Christopher know exactly what he must contribute. Christopher, on receiving made-man status, reports to Paulie, who tells him that he must clear six grand. Paulie is clear about the results he expects. Shortly thereafter, Christopher presents Paulie with four grand; Paulie responds that this number is unacceptable. In true Christopher style, he tells Paulie that he needs a couple of days to come up with the rest but "he's learned a valuable lesson." Paulie doesn't want to hear any of his excuses. He says, "I'm not running a school here, kid." Though Paulie gives him the requested additional time, he makes Christopher pay the price for his poor performance; he charges him a late fee of an additional two grand. Thus, Paulie provides us with an addendum to the coaching lesson: Enforce negative consequences when expectations aren't met.

What It Takes to Get Ahead

Go into any organization and you are bound to hear employees grousing about not getting promoted or not getting ahead as quickly as they would like. For many, getting ahead remains a mystery, even if they've had long and repeated conversations with their bosses about the promotion process. Unfortunately, their bosses have coached them using platitudes and empty promises. They've told them things such as:

- Just keep working hard and your time will come.
- I don't know, go ask human resources.
- I am not sure I can put into words what you have to do, but I will know it when I see it.
- I have been fighting for your promotion but my boss (or human resources) said no. I guess maybe we don't have the money right now.

In the first two seasons, Christopher was constantly campaigning to become a made man. Although Tony never completely spells out the criteria for becoming a made man, he informs Christopher that a set number of spots become available when the higher bosses "open up the books." At this point, the capos give their recommendations. During the show's first season, Christopher raises the issue even after being chastised for hijacking Junior's trucks. Tony is clear to Christopher that the ". . . books are closed and we are not accepting new members." After giving

Christopher direction about making restitution to Junior over the hijacking, Tony tells him, ". . . you have a reputation for immaturity and it won't be improved by not paying the tributes the acting boss demands of you." In this instance, Tony will not support him being a made man because he continues to be a loose cannon and the others will not respect him if this behavior continues.

After another incident with a hijacked truck that Christopher failed to stop, Tony offers even more specific advice about what it takes to get ahead: "Did you do anything to stop it [the hijacking]? Did you offer any guidance? What do we mean when we say leadership?" Tony is teaching Christopher a valuable lesson; he's telling him that a made man would not have simply denied involvement in the hijacking but would have stepped in and stopped an action he knew the bosses wouldn't countenance. Like any good coach, Tony was providing "just-in-time" learning, using a real business problem to teach Christopher about promotion criteria. In this way, he was focusing not only on Christopher's current performance but also his potential for a future leadership role.

Tony is tremendously astute when it comes to coaching difficult but talented people. Ralph, for instance, is a great producer but a "difficult" person to work with. Ralph complains to Tony about not being promoted to captain, and Tony handles the confrontation brilliantly. At some point, most leaders face the dilemma of either promoting an individual star who is a lousy team player or risk losing this star if he isn't promoted.

When Tony passes over Ralph for captain, he sits down and tells Ralph the news, explaining that he is promoting Gigi to captain over him. He talks to Ralph about his bad temper and cites several examples of poor decisions. Ralph responds angrily, reciting the familiar lament of how he "busts his butt" and brings in a lot of money. Later, Ralph again brings up the topic of his promotion, though his timing is not particularly good because he recently beat a stripper to death. Tony wisely reminds him of his bad judgment, telling him he disrespected the Bing and that is why he was passed over for captain.

Unlike many leaders, Tony didn't coach Ralph by making false promises just to retain him a bit longer. He also didn't verbally attack him in an attempt to bully him into behaving. Instead, he was honest with Ralph about why he was passed over and made the criteria for promotion clear.

This is the tough type of conversation most leaders can relate to. Tony chooses to let Ralph know where he stands and what he needs to do differently to get ahead. Certainly Tony realizes that Ralph is not going to be receptive to this message and will initially react negatively, but Tony's bigger-picture goal is to develop Ralph's leadership abilities, and he knows this conversation is necessary for Ralph's development.

HOW TO BE IMPERFECTLY EFFECTIVE

As you're reading this, you may be having trouble reconciling Tony's aggressiveness with the notion of a good coach. While instilling fear is one of Tony's coaching techniques and he does have a tendency to be less than effusive (which especially bothers Christopher), Tony also knows who he's coaching. He recognizes that his direct reports are hard-edged, tough criminals who require a certain amount of intimidation; it goes with the territory. When you coach, you need to know your audience. Leaders learn that a group of young, cutting-edge techies needs to be coached differently than a group of veteran salespeople does. Tony's intimidating style works with his crew because they accept this style as integral to being a boss, and they also know that they can fight back (within limits) when Tony loses his temper and not be punished for it. They also are aware that Tony will eventually cool down and be willing to listen to reason.

Because no coach is perfect, you can expect to make mistakes when dealing with your people. You're going to say and do the wrong things when coaching people, but if you've talked straight with them, clarified your expectations, and explained what's needed to get ahead, they'll forgive your errors and remain coachable. These three coaching strengths will teach people that you can be counted on. When you're trying to coach a direct report in a crisis situation or when she's facing a major career decision, you know that she'll rely on you for direction and support. Who were Paulie and Christopher waiting for to save them when they were lost in the woods in the "Pine Barrens" episode? When Christopher becomes a made man, Tony tells him, "You bring your problems to Tony, he will solve them."

Part of being an effective coach is getting your people to rely on you when they're in trouble, to come to you for help rather than wait for you to see problems and intervene. Tony's crew may be afraid of their boss, but they're not afraid to ask him for help.

To help you coach in an imperfectly effective way, do the following:

1. Describe the general characteristics of the people you're coaching:
   - Are they tough as nails or soft as marshmallows?
   - Are they Young Turks or old traditionalists?
   - Are they highly ambitious or more interested in maintaining the status quo?
   - Do they have thick skins or are they vulnerable types?
2. Given the general characteristics of your people, try to tailor your coaching style to these characteristics; determine how tough you can be, how much one-on-one coaching they'll tolerate, and so on. Though each person has his or her own issues and needs to be handled somewhat differently, they all possess certain general traits that can guide your coaching efforts.
3. Assess honestly whether your people readily come to you in times of trouble. If they do, great. If not, you need to fo-

cus your coaching efforts on being straight with them, clarifying expectations and establishing promotion criteria.

4. List your weaknesses as a coach. Here are some common weaknesses:
   - Unwilling to confront poor performance
   - Difficulty dealing with personality conflicts
   - Poor listening skills
   - Lack of knowledge about an area relevant to coachee's problem
   - Lack of skill in assessing performance
   - Finding certain types of direct reports difficult to coach
   - Missing the authority to help direct reports solve a problem or take advantage of an opportunity
   - Being too critical
   - Struggling to offer positive feedback
   - Putting the needs of the coachee first

5. Create at least two "resources" who can supplement your coaching, based on your weaknesses. They can be peers, bosses, or outside coaches. The key is to fill in your coaching blanks with these two people.

DON'T CONFUSE COACHING WITH COMFORTING

All executives can take a cue from Tony when it comes to putting a little backbone into their coaching. Too often, leaders coach as if people were as fragile as the most delicate glass. They use coaching purely to demonstrate sympathy and empathy. They listen actively and generally allow others to pour their hearts out. Certainly empathy and listening are important aspects of coaching, but as Tony well knows, direct reports can be as manipulative as Christopher and as needy as Paulie, and sometimes you have to give 'em a little smack (figuratively, of course) instead of sympathetic pats. Being direct with direct reports should be your mantra. Tony doesn't mince words and neither should you.

You'll recall our earlier example of when Christopher shot a civilian in the foot and Tony chewed him out. Imagine how a touchy-feely boss might have dealt with this situation using the five-step coaching model:

Step 1. (*Establish rapport*) "Hey Christopher, can I talk to you for a minute. How are things going? How are you feeling about things these days? I wanted to talk with you about a couple of things. Okay?"

Step 2. (*Specify behavior but leave room for an explanation*) "Now, this may not be true and if it is I'm sure there must be a good explanation. Someone mentioned that you shot a civilian in the foot because you had to wait in line for buns." (*At this point the leader would let Christopher talk.*)

Step 3. (*Listen with empathy*) The leader would listen to Christopher's explanation of his behavior.

Step 4. (*Discuss the standard of behavior and the impact the individual's behavior had on you*) "Shooting civilians is unacceptable behavior. When you do this type of behavior, Christopher, I get upset because we are under the microscope with the Feds and this makes us stand out."

Step 5. (*Enhance self-esteem of the person*) "Christopher, you are a great earner and a great guy. I trust that we will not see this type of behavior again."

As you can see, this coach has good intentions but bad effects. His Christopher won't get the message. Or at the very least, the message will be watered down by his excess verbiage, attempts to stroke the guy's ego, and mild reprimand. While this person may feel listened to, he won't realize that he made a major error and he is likely to repeat this mistake in the future.

TONY ON THE NEED FOR
EXECUTIVE DEVELOPMENT

"Why don't you fuckin' grow up?"

As a coach, you need to follow Tony's lead and practice compassionate criticism. When someone does something wrong or is pursuing the wrong course of action, you need to coach them back to the right course with firm though empathetic suggestions. Tony let Christopher know that behavior such as shooting civilians is unacceptable, he asks Christopher a series of questions and probes to discover what is behind his erratic behavior. At no time does he excuse the behavior, but he does try to delve more deeply into the issues that Christopher is facing. Tony is able to balance the toughness of the message delivery with the softness of his concern for Christopher's self-destructive behavior. As Christopher talks about his feelings about life, Tony turns to him, gently touches his head and puts himself in Christopher's shoes by saying, "Look at you. I bet you're sleeping all the time?" Christopher wonders whether he might have cancer like Jackie. Tony, sounding a bit like Dr. Melfi, asks, "Does this word *cancer* pop into your mind a lot, a little bit . . . what?" At no time, does he fall into the common coaching trap of dispensing advice so that the focus is no longer on the individual being coached. Coaches do their people a disservice when they pontificate or talk about how they would handle a given situation.

Let's look at two versions of how the second part of this conversation with Christopher might have gone if Tony were a different type of coach:

Version #1:

Christopher: "Let me explain. I am struggling with the regularness of life. What's it all about?"

Tony: "I know just what you mean. I have some of those very same questions. Why just the other day, I was asking Carmela what we are doing here on this earth. What is the purpose of our existence? What does it mean?

Don't worry Christopher, everything will be all right. These feelings will pass. It's just a phase you are going through."

Version #2:

Christopher: "Let me explain. I am struggling with the regularness of life. What's it all about?"

Tony: "Come on. You are not serious. Look at all that you have to live for. You have your whole life in front of you. You're a great kid. Forget about it."

In both of these scenarios, the leader had good intent—he was concentrating on comforting—but was never truly listening or trying to focus on Christopher's needs. In the first version, Tony was trying to show empathy by talking about a similar situation he faced. This only served, however, to shift the focus away from Christopher and onto Tony. Referring to Carmela's problem isn't relevant. In the second version, Tony basically invalidates and discounts Christopher's feelings. Whether Christopher's feelings are justified or not, these are feelings that are troubling him and getting in the way of his performance.

If Tony were to walk in the door of a typical organization and witness the way bosses coach people, he would be aghast. In fact, if he were to see the extent to which bosses are afraid to tell people the truth about their performance and what they need to do to improve, he might ask, "What the fuck is going on here?" Organizations today frequently implement strategies to drive more openness and candor into the workplace. In annual employee surveys, however, the items scoring the lowest are often ones relating to feedback, coaching, and performance-evaluation clarity. Leaders struggle mightily to tell direct reports that they're not cutting it, fearing the resistance that Tony got from Christopher (or the tears they might receive from someone else). To "help" leaders talk straight to their people, some organizations introduce forced distribution or forced ranking processes (bell-shaped curves with so many individuals in the high rankings and so many individuals in the low rankings) to their performance-management systems. These processes "force" leaders to differentiate the performance of their employees. Before this system was implemented in one organization, it was rating more than 60 percent of its employees as top performers at a time when the business results clearly did not warrant such a rating, and it was tolerating subpar or marginal performance. Tony would approve of this forced rating system, knowing that it would provide the impetus for candid coaching conversations.

Striking a balance between being a Bobby Knight–type coach and a pushover type isn't easy. The latter tends to be regarded as nice and easy to work for, but he usually doesn't deliver results or helps his direct reports grow. The former gets results but at the price of losing some of his best people and creating terrible morale problems.

TONY ON COACHING WITH COMPASSION

"I got some news you're not gonna like."

Tony seems to have mastered the Zen of coaching, in that he has found a balancing point, one in which he is paradoxically tough and gentle simultaneously. As Junior said in a "coaching" session with Tony, "There is no answer. You steer the ship as best you can." In his "performance discussions," Tony is always very clear that it is "business not personal." He is careful to focus on the specifics of the situation and what was not done well versus the individual. Although he doesn't care for Christopher's excuses and lets him know it, he is a good listener, open to a discussion of the facts, and able to communicate that he cares. If appropriate, he will let you know that he has been in your shoes. After most of his tense "coaching sessions," Tony always ends them with a hug. For Tony this is his way of reassuring people that the relationship is fine, even if a specific screwup isn't. In effect, he is saying, "The incident is behind us, we'll move on, and I still care for you."

TONY'S INSTA-COACH TIPS
How to Coach Fast, Efficiently, and Effectively

One of the worst things about coaching is that it can be an enormously time-consuming, energy-draining experience. More than one executive has found herself entangled in a complex, seemingly endless series of meetings with a direct report who just can't seem to get it together. At times, coaching feels akin to a never-ending task, because problems recycle without solution. Just when you think you've coached one person in a helpful way, another issue surfaces and you're back to square one.

One of the great assets of Tony's coaching style is its speed and pragmatism. Not only does Tony cut to the chase when he's helping his people deal with issues but he does so without making them feel like he's giving them the bum's rush. If Tony could advise you how to deal with the ten most common coaching problems you face, here's what he might suggest.

Problem #1

You have a direct report who always offers excuses for missed deadlines and sloppy execution. She never accepts responsibility for her actions. When you talk to her and try to explain what she did wrong and how she might correct it, she provides very reasonable explanations of why something went wrong, and you're left questioning yourself. When you think about it, though, you see the pattern of behavior and know she's investing more energy in coming up with excuses than in doing the work.

Tip. The next time she starts offering excuses, don't act like a wuss and go all apologetic. Interrupt her in midsentence. Raise your voice so she knows you mean business. Slap the table for emphasis. And tell her you don't want to hear one more excuse. Not now. Not ever again.

Problem #2

Your talented direct report is a lone ranger and works poorly with other members of your team. People complain they can't work with him because he's so abrasive and refuses to share information. You've pushed him to change, but you're afraid to push him too hard because he's talented enough that he could easily get another job.

Tip. Make up your mind if you're willing to risk losing him. If you are, let him know the impact he's having and that this is not the way to become a "made" executive. If he's too valuable to lose, then keep him away from everyone else and give him projects he can work on by himself.

Problem #3

For the third time in the past few months, a direct report has complained to you about not receiving a promotion she feels she richly deserves. You just don't think she's ready to take on a more responsible position—which you've hinted at—but she refuses to pick up on the hint and is clearly resentful, which is impacting her work and the morale of your group.

Tip. Stop pussyfooting around. Tell her she isn't ready and if she keeps whining about it, she'll never be ready. Don't give her a load of crap about how there aren't any openings or how your boss put the kabosh on it. Let her know you're standing in her way and why. Then tell her what she needs to do so you'll be willing to give her promotion your blessing.

Problem #4

You're working with a veteran employee, someone who has been with you for years, but his performance has slipped recently. You've had a good relationship and he obviously feels like he's secure because of this long-standing association. He's coasting, perhaps because he only has a few years before retirement, but he's hurting your results. When you talk to him about his performance, you feel uneasy, as if you're being disloyal to him in some way, and so you back off.

Tip. Be straight with him. If you think he's a good guy who's been loyal, you owe him big time, and you aren't doing him any favors by pretending he's cutting it. Tell him what he is doing wrong and what he needs to do to save his job. Yeah, it's tough, and he might not like you leveling with him, but if he's smart, he'll figure you have his best interests at heart.

Problem #5

You have someone working for you who is very nice and tries hard, but you suspect she's wrong for the job; her skills and attitude just don't mesh with the position's responsibilities. You believe you're responsible because you assigned her the job, so combined with her niceness and hard work, you don't feel you can tell her that it's not working out.

Tip. So do you think it would be better if you both get the ax? There are lots of nice, hardworking stiffs in the world, only you don't want them working for you. Maybe you can find her a position that's a better fit. Whatever, just don't sit there twiddling your thumbs. The longer you wait, the harder it's going to be, and the more damage she's going to do.

Problem #6

The merit pool for increases was small this year and you had to give a senior member of your group (but not your top performer) a lower-than-average increase, even though he made valuable contributions. When you give him his increase, he becomes irate.

Tip. Okay, life isn't fair, and you can't control everything. Tell him that. You also should acknowledge his contributions and maybe reward him some other way—a day off, a tip on a fixed horse race, that type of thing. Be straight about what he needs to do differently next year. Don't keep information about raises a secret like the Feds are tapping your conversation and they'll throw you in the slammer if you breathe a word about this stuff.

Problem #7

You have a usually reliable performer who is going through a rough patch because of a divorce. She's caught up in the emotion and the details of a messy breakup. Still, your group has had to carry her for two months, and you don't know how much longer you can do so before the group's performance is hurt.

Tip. Believe me, I know how this type of thing can mess up your mind. Talk to her as a human being, not just as her boss. Forget the line between personal and professional. The right thing to do is to listen to her talk about what's bothering her, and be compassionate. Maybe even suggest she get help through Employee Assistance. You've got to watch things so they don't hurt your team, but cut her some slack. The odds are she'll get through the divorce okay and pretty soon she'll be contributing like she did before.

Problem #8

You've got a top performer who is starting to top you. He's excelling at everything you give him and making other people around him better. You naturally feel threatened and wonder if his superior performance will make your bosses wonder why he doesn't have your job. You're thinking about talking to him and telling him to "pace himself."

Tip. You got an insecurity problem or what? Are your bosses a bunch of numskulls who don't get that your leadership is what is helping this guy do such a bang-up job? You should talk to him, but tell him to keep it up; pat him on the back and find ways to reward him. He might get your job, but only after you've been promoted yourself for being the type of leader who can grow his people.

Problem #9

You have a young direct report who has gotten off to a great start, which has also resulted in a growing arrogance that you and others find off-putting. Just as important, she is overconfident to the point that she is getting sloppy—she isn't as thorough as she was when she first joined your group. You want to rein her in without discouraging her, but you're not sure how to do so.

Tip. Don't lecture her; don't tell her how it was when you were young. These kids hate that stuff. Instead, let her know what others think about the way she'd been acting. Let them tell her she's been sloppy, that she's walking around with a stick up her butt. She can't argue with the facts, and she'll take it better if you tell her all the good things she's been doing to balance out the bad.

Problem #10

Your boss comes to you for advice. He's excited about a white paper he wants to publish on the company Web site concerning the future of your industry, but he wants your feedback before doing so. You find that although he has included a lot of good ideas in the paper, he also reaches conclusions that will discourage employees—he talks about how the industry's golden age is over—never to return. You wonder if you should burst his bubble and tell him why you don't think his paper should be published, or if you should assume that he really doesn't want any feedback that isn't approving.

Tip. Unless he's a weasel, he asked you because he respects your opinion; he'd be disappointed if you were anything less than honest. Of course, you don't want to be an idiot and say something like, "This stinks!" Tell him what concerns you about the white paper; lay out the downside for him. Then volunteer to help him edit it so it eliminates the downside.

COACHING IS MORE THAN A ONE-ON-ONE ACTIVITY

Too often, coaches forget that the ramifications of a coaching exchange extend beyond the two people having a conversation. It's a formal organizational activity, not just a personal dialogue. As such, you need to coach like your organization's reputation is on the line. Leaders often don't realize that what they say and do in individual coaching sessions sends a strong message about organizational values and the behaviors they're willing to tolerate. Though Tony eventually promotes Ralph, he resists this action for a long time, because he knows this promotion will send the wrong message. Ralph is a sleaze, and Tony knows that Ralph's values are different from his.

If your values and your organization's values are synonymous, the key to good coaching is being open and honest. If you tell a direct report how you truly feel, you'll be sending the right message both for the individual and the organization.

TONY'S COACHING AHA!

You gotta be straight with your people or they're never gonna be straight with you.

5

GIVE IT TO MY FACE

Receiving Feedback

Our most effective leaders are
like Tony—they're fearless about sharing their weaknesses and exposing their vulnerabilities. These leaders continually ask for
feedback on how they are doing and want to know what they
should change to be more effective. Just as significant, they listen
to this feedback and adjust their behavior if such change is warranted. They don't surround themselves with yes-men. Instead,
they're sufficiently comfortable in their skins that their inner circle includes individuals who challenge their thinking.

Tony can dish it out, but he can also take it, a hallmark of a
truly effective leader. Though he makes a great effort to avoid
physical vulnerability, he allows himself to be emotionally vulnerable. Not only does he want to hear the bad news and the criti-
cisms, but he encourages people to give him both.

You have to be tough to take feedback, and Tony is as tough
as they come. No one likes to hear a direct report tell him that
he's not communicating clearly or for a partner to tell him that
he messed up. Tony doesn't like to hear these things, but there's

a big difference between not liking it and not allowing it. Like any powerful leader, Tony has a healthy ego, and as a result he doesn't enjoy learning that he isn't doing as good a job as he thought he was. A healthy ego, as opposed to an overinflated ego, can tolerate the pain to reap the rewards of feedback. Because Tony knows he's a good leader, he also knows that the majority of feedback he receives will be positive. Even when Tony receives negative feedback, he generally is able to tolerate it better than most leaders because he knows his crew is offering to help him improve the organization. Leaders lacking confidence in their own abilities are the ones most likely to forbid honesty or be afraid to make themselves vulnerable.

TONY ON THE NEED TO TAKE EGO OUT OF THE FEEDBACK EQUATION

"It's business."

More than ever before, we need leaders who are strong enough to tolerate criticism and bad news. In open, fast-moving cultures, leaders don't have the luxury of cutting themselves off from critical information. The best leaders are familiar with their strengths and weaknesses and don't make bad decisions because they're laboring under illusions about themselves. Receptivity to feedback makes this objectivity and information flow possible.

GRANTING FEEDBACK PRIVILEGES TO THOSE WHO DESERVE THEM

Obviously, Tony isn't a masochist. Being receptive to feedback isn't the same as pinning a kick-me sign on your rear end. Tony chooses his feedback partners carefully—he selects those who will level with him—and they include his captains, Christopher, Junior, Dr. Melfi, and some family members. He also sets parameters; he expects the feedback to be delivered respectfully and with the best interests of the organization at heart.

Tony encourages feedback by creating an environment of openness and candor. Within this environment, he establishes certain rules—he is the boss, has the last word, and when he says he's heard enough, he expects the other person to shut up—but he expects and promotes debate, disagreement, and straight talk. In fact, Tony is almost fearless in his ability to accept whatever feedback is thrown his way from his guys. If Tony were to formalize his feedback philosophy, it might read as follows:

- Feedback is nothing to be afraid of—it only hurts when you allow it to hurt. It's business.
- You can always reject the feedback.
- People provide you with feedback because they care and want you to succeed, or conversely, they don't want you to get hurt.
- Create opportunities for people to give you feedback to your face; better they should tell you directly what they think rather than whisper it behind your back.
- Don't shoot the messenger, even though you might feel like shooting him; settle down, listen, and learn. And tell yourself again not to shoot him.

Let's look at Tony's feedback philosophy in action. When Jackie Aprile was in the hospital dying of cancer, Tony and Junior's crews started vying for power and control in the certain event of Jackie's death. Out of respect for both Jackie and Junior, Tony at times would acquiesce control to Junior over certain business transactions. Immediately following Jackie's death, Christopher tells Tony, "I represent you out there and I'm tired of putting my tail between my legs . . . If you don't do something I have to question your leadership." For Tony, who prides himself on not "laying down" for anyone, Christopher's feedback must have been a tremendous jolt to his ego. No doubt, Tony's initial instinct was to go for Christopher's throat. He quickly backs off, though, for three reasons: He trusts Christopher; he knows Christopher has no self-serving motive to say what he said; and most important, he reminds himself that Christopher cares for him and the last thing Christopher wants is for Tony's reputation to be sullied. From that point, Tony sets in motion the plan for Junior to be the boss but with Tony calling the shots.

TONY ON THE NEED FOR FRANKNESS
WHEN REQUESTING FEEDBACK

"You gotta problem with me?"

Tony created the right environment for Christopher to give him feedback. Let's examine how Tony displayed superb leadership skills in absorbing this feedback.

First, Tony didn't respond to what Christopher said with excuses about why he didn't go up against Junior. Instead of getting bogged down in offering his rationale, he realized the "why" was irrelevant and the damage had been done. This response prevented Christopher from becoming defensive and backing off the truth as he saw it.

Second, Tony did try to shoot the messenger—he grabbed Christopher by the throat—but he quickly calmed down, listened, and focused on what Christopher was saying without judging Christopher.

Third, Tony set the stage for Christopher to be honest through his consistent behavior. In the past when Tony received unpleasant feedback, he would explode, calm down, listen, and avoid shooting the messenger. His people could count on Tony not to be vindictive. He had made it clear that he valued honesty and truth, and for this reason, Christopher wasn't afraid to be honest.

It's not simply that Tony creates an environment where his key people feel that he wants feedback; Tony makes specific requests for feedback when he knows it's important to make these requests.

The classic example of this occurred when too many people knew that Tony was seeing a psychiatrist. Acutely aware that he had to clear the air with his key people and get on with business, he calls Christopher, Paulie, and Sil together and says, "I need to tell you something . . . I want you to hear it from me and not some asshole on the street. About four or five months ago I started seeing a psychiatrist because I was passing out." He pauses and then says, "Come on, give it to me. Give it to my face, come on." When they don't say anything, he reassures them that no business was discussed during the sessions and no names were mentioned. Finally, he says, "Ask me now, 'cause we're not discussing it again." He pauses and then Paulie talks about seeing a psychiatrist a while back. Sil makes a comment. Christopher, though, is silent and Tony directly addresses him with, "What about you? You gotta problem with this?" Christopher simply walks away, unable to articulate his feelings.

Tony's feedback gestalt was effective for several reasons:

- By talking about this subject openly, he made the first move and thus retained control of the situation.
- He showed his respect for his people by telling them the news first before they heard it "on the street."
- He also gave his people the information (no business or names were discussed) so they could defend him on the street if others started talking about it or asking questions. His people had all the facts and could talk credibly if challenged by others.
- By being proactive, he mitigated the potential for gossip behind his back if one of them heard or suspected what was going on. A leader who is gossiped about tends to be a leader who doesn't invite feedback (gossip needs an information-poor environment in which to thrive).
- Tony gave them the chance to say whatever they needed to say in front of him, providing him with an opportunity for rebuttal or to address specific points.
- He asked for feedback in a very human way. Tony took a risk with his admission that he was seeing a therapist, ex-

posing his weakness and communicating that he wasn't the perfect leader. The downside of such a move is that his people realize he is not all-powerful and all-knowing, that he is as vulnerable as they are. In Tony's culture—and in many corporate cultures, for that matter—this can open you up to attack and decrease loyalty. The upside, however, more than makes up for this potential negative. When leaders humanize themselves, they earn far greater loyalty from most of their people; it is much easier to have a strong relationship with a human being than with a demigod. It is also better that leaders humanize themselves than have others reveal their weaknesses. This is the difference between someone admitting he has a problem and seeking help versus a banner headline in the next day's paper exposing his problem. We tend to admire the former action and are shocked and angered by the latter.

- After Tony told them about the therapy, he waited for them to respond. He let others talk without interrupting them or trying to correct their impressions. Most important of all, Tony did not make excuses for his behavior or become defensive. He knows that he probably disappointed Christopher, but he let him walk away. The most positive thing Tony did—and what many leaders fail to do when receiving feedback—is demonstrating not only that he was listening, but that he "heard."

ARE YOU FEEDBACK-FRIENDLY?

Most leaders don't practice Tony's feedback gestalt. To a greater or lesser extent, they stifle feedback. Sometimes they create environments where people are reluctant to tell them the truth. Sometimes they encourage feedback but don't really listen to what people tell them. And sometimes they say or do things that throw the feedback back in the faces of the people who provided it.

Think about whether you are receptive to feedback. If you're not, you need to identify the cause. The following are the ten most common reasons leaders reject or avoid receiving feedback. Determine which ones apply to you and then implement the suggestions for overcoming your feedback-averse response.

1. The truth may hurt.
2. You might have to acknowledge that you are not perfect.
3. The feedback does not make sense—they obviously don't understand you or your intentions.
4. You might have to change and you lack the time or energy to do so.
5. You don't care.
6. Their comments are motivated by their dislike of you, so you can dismiss what they say.
7. Acknowledging the feedback means acknowledging you messed up.
8. You might have to engage in a painful conversation.
9. It will open old wounds.
10. You don't respect the person(s) giving you the feedback.

How Tony Can Help You Overcome Your Feedback-Averse Reactions

1. **The truth may hurt.** As Tony might say, "Yeah, but it's better than a sharp stick in the eye." Which, figuratively speaking, is exactly what you'll get if you ignore feedback. Think about Tony's inner strength and how well it serves him. If you're strong enough, you can take some criticism and bad news. Not to be insulting, but Tony's thick skin allows him to absorb a certain amount of hurtful feedback. Develop this thick skin by training your inner voice to repeat, "It's business, not personal." This inner voice can help take your ego out of the equation momentarily, giving you the space

you need to process whatever feedback comes your way. Remember that this will help you become a better leader, even if the feedback stings for a second.

2. You might have to acknowledge that you are not perfect. You're probably under the influence of the traditional leadership model, one in which people in power weren't allowed to show weakness. This may have worked 30 years ago but not now. Think of your imperfections as your strengths. Tony certainly has weaknesses—a bad temper, hubris, a sometimes cruel sense of humor, and so on—but he usually doesn't mind when others point out his flaws. Remember, leadership isn't about being perfect; it's about doing the best you can despite your imperfections.

3. The feedback does not make sense—they obviously don't understand you or your intentions. It doesn't make sense only because you're not really listening to what people are telling you. They may be wrong, but it's worth trying to figure out if that's the case rather than immediately dismissing what they say because you assume they don't understand you. Tony sometimes gets frustrated when he thinks people have misunderstood his intent, but he doesn't allow that frustration to stop him from listening. Wait until you've received all the feedback and then determine if they misunderstood your intentions. In addition, be aware that a lot of people don't give two figs about your intentions if your actions had a negative impact. They're giving you flak because your decision hurt them in some way. Therefore, focus on how your behavior must change to remedy a problem rather than waste time trying to justify your actions.

4. You might have to change and you lack the time or energy to do so. Tony is astonishingly adaptable. He can shift positions on a dime when the information dictates change. Yes, change takes time and energy, but it's what allows Tony to create alliances with former enemies and recognize emerging opportunities before others do.

5. You don't care. Typically, leaders don't care what others have to tell them because they're brimming with self-confidence and believe they know everything they need to make good decisions. In a world where new information is being created every second, though, no leader knows enough. As confident as Tony is, he recognizes that he needs to depend on his crew for information—there's just too much happening for him to keep tabs on everything. No matter how confident you are, you're probably not as confident as Tony, and he recognizes that he needs to listen to others to be a good leader.

6. Their comments are motivated by their dislike of you, so you can dismiss what they say. At his paranoid worst, Tony sometimes thinks this way. Fortunately, he quickly snaps out of it, realizing that some of the most valuable information can come from his enemies. The key isn't to dismiss their feedback, but to sift through it for valuable nuggets of information. Tony is an expert at interpreting what's behind people's words, their motivations, and interests. Even if people dislike you and that is skewing what they tell you, see if you can read between the lines and learn something from their slanted perspectives.

7. Acknowledging the feedback means acknowledging you messed up. Tony hates admitting he's wrong, but he is capable of doing so. He seems to go through a process where at first he rejects the feedback indicating he messed up, losing his temper in the process, and then a little bit later, he pushes his ego aside and deals objectively with the information he's received. Take a cue from Tony and do the same thing (without losing your temper, if you can avoid it). In other words, take the negative information in, shove it to the side with your skepticism, and then review it again when the "insult" isn't as fresh or painful.

8. You might have to engage in a painful conversation. It's all too common for executives to avoid specific types of discussions with people because they know they're going to be dealing with difficult topics. For instance, they avoid a discussion of a recent performance review, not just because they gave someone a bad review but because they anticipate negative feedback about how they conducted the review. In most instances, though, these painful conversations are part of leadership territory. Tony doesn't enjoy telling Junior he's made a mistake or correcting a "sensitive" member of his crew, anticipating that he's going to be on the receiving end of negative feedback after he says what he needs to. Many times, though, these painful conversations clear the air, getting angry feelings into the open. The key for leaders is to control the discussion so that the feedback—and the emotions—doesn't hurt the relationship.

9. It will open old wounds. Tony, like many leaders, has a lot of bodies (both physical and emotional) he'd rather remain buried. Feedback can unearth these bodies. Avoiding feedback can help you avoid hearing the type of news that makes you feel sad, guilty, or angry. Yet you also avoid listening to news you might be able to use. In most instances, though, you need to grit your teeth and listen to wound-opening information by being fully in the present. As much as Tony nurses old wounds, he is able to keep his ears open even when the information hurts him because of something that happened in the past.

10. You don't respect the person(s) giving you the feedback. Tony is skilled at feigning respect for people to get them to talk to him. He may not respect Ralph, but he values him both as an income and an information source (at least until he kills him). One of the big mistakes many leaders make is accepting feedback only from their cronies, from an inner circle of like-minded individuals. Everyone can use 360-degree feedback, and if you limit it to 90 degrees, you're limiting your knowledge.

TWO KEYS TO DETERMINE THE VALUE OF THE INFORMATION AND THE IDEAS RECEIVED

As a general rule, the more powerful the leader, the less willing he is to accept feedback. CEOs, for instance, tend to have more difficulty receiving and reflecting on feedback than younger, less senior leaders. This makes perfect sense, for CEOs rightly feel that they've been at it longer and doing it better than others, and they trust their instincts because these instincts have carried them so far. It's not that they don't trust others; it's simply that they have so much faith in their own ability to get things done.

Tony is this type of CEO, but unlike most top executives, Tony invites and evaluates a constant flow of responses to what he does and says. Lou Gerstner, former CEO of IBM, was known to ask for feedback from everyone, including people he was riding with on the elevator. Tony maximizes the value of this process by:

- Asking questions about the feedback of himself and others
- Absorbing the feedback and not responding to it immediately

The former method allows Tony to filter the feedback through his own analysis and the analysis of those whose opinions he values. For instance, in the show's third season, Artie decides to supplement the income from his restaurant with a little shylocking. He makes a loan to his hostess's brother who wants to finance a French liqueur distributorship in the United States. The brother fails to pay up and Artie stumbles in his attempt to collect his money even after threatening to "break the brother's knees." Tony ends up assuming the loan, and as partial payment, Tony strikes a deal with Artie to eat at Artie's restaurant for free. Artie gives Tony some tough feedback about this experience. He suggests that Tony knew this would be the outcome, insinuating that he might have even planned it. More specifically, Artie tells Tony, "You can see 20 moves ahead. Your mind goes through all the permutations . . . the worst case was you eat for free."

Later, Tony asks Dr. Melfi, "Am I that kind of person?" This feedback upset Tony, for he did not perceive himself as so crassly manipulative, especially when friends such as Artie were involved. From his perspective, he was simply trying to help Artie. Tony questions himself and others. He seriously wonders if he was unconsciously trying to gain from Artie's loss. After all, this was his strategy when he allowed Dave, the owner of the sporting goods store, to play in the executive card game. Tony knew that if Dave lost big in the game, the store would be his. Nonetheless, Tony doesn't like to picture himself as a deceiver of friends. Whether Tony chooses to change his behavior isn't the issue, it's that the feedback that Artie has given him "tees up" the option for him to consider. It allows him to be a self-aware leader, which will help him make decisions without being overly influenced by his inner demons.

Tony's ability to absorb negative feedback without blowing up or engaging the person who supplied the feedback in rancorous debate is astonishing. For someone with Tony's power and his bad temper, this self-control is admirable. No doubt, it's what encourages so many people in his life to tell him the truth and be honest about what's bothering them. After Tony calls Vin (the gambler and FBI police detective who owes Pussy a great deal of money) a "degenerate gambler with a badge," Vin gives Tony some feedback: "You have an amazing ability to sum up a man's whole life in a single sentence." Tony just shrugs his shoulders and continues on.

Richie Aprile is another guy who does not hold his tongue in Tony's presence. Richie believes that Tony has disrespected him ever since he has been released from prison; that Tony owes him greater respect because he is a made man. After a dispute during the executive card game, Richie tells Tony, "I'm getting sick of this holier-than-thou act and I'm not the only one." After Tony eggs him on with, ". . . well if anyone wants to make a move,"

Richie comes right back with, "Don't get so fuckin' dramatic. Sometimes you act like you're in a different business." Again, Tony just shrugs off this insulting comment. He refuses to become defensive or berate Richie. As a result, Richie and others in the room are encouraged to speak their minds in the future.

TONY ON OFFERING HONEST EXPLANATIONS IN RESPONSE TO MISTAKES MADE

"I have no defense, that's how I was parented."

GIVE-IT-TO-MY-FACE TECHNIQUES

When is the last time your people criticized something you did or said?

If they do say something negative to you, are you likely to take their heads off?

When you receive feedback, do you take the time and clear the emotional space to reflect on it objectively and deeply?

Most leaders respond that people don't usually criticize them; that they did indeed bark at someone when they said something that opposed their point of view; and that they often let negative or disturbing information go in one ear and out the other because they don't give it much credence.

Making the transition to a more feedback-friendly stance takes a little bit of time and effort. In fact, Tony over the course of the shows seems to have gradually become more responsive to feedback, in part because of his sessions with Dr. Melfi who has encouraged his growing self-awareness. In addition, failure often makes people more receptive to feedback; it creates self-doubt in leaders who previously had no doubts, and they become more willing to listen to what others have to say to them.

To help you build an environment in which people are willing to level with you and you're willing to treat their information and ideas seriously, I've created the following four approaches:

I. A FEW SMALL, EASY-TO-TAKE ACTIONS CAN GET THE FEEDBACK ROLLING IN:

1. At the next meeting you lead, ask someone you trust to observe you during the meeting and note things you did well and things that, as Tony might say, you fucked up. After the meeting ask him to tell you what he observed. If he is not immediately forthcoming about areas for improvement, use Tony's technique of persistent questioning. Ask him: "Are you sure there isn't something?" or "Remember when I _____, how do you think that went over?" You may not receive a lot of feedback the first time, but that leads to the second step.
2. At the next presentation you give, repeat step #1.
3. At home, ask a family member what's one thing she would like you to do differently.

II. AFTER YOU GET USED TO THIS PROCESS, TAKE SOME BIGGER STEPS:

1. At the next meeting or presentation where your boss is present, let him know beforehand that you would like him to give you feedback on how you did.
2. If you are not sure how you are doing at work or if you have not received feedback lately from your boss, tell her that you would like to schedule some time to talk with her about your performance. Once you are in the meeting, focus on things you are doing well and things that need improvement. If your boss is not that forthcoming, ask her what the one thing is that she would like you to do differently.
3. If you have never had a performance review from your boss, ask for one. Every company usually has a process for this but many employees don't take advantage of it.
4. In individual meetings with your direct reports, do as former New York City Mayor Ed Koch would do and ask, "How am I doing?"

III. START COLLECTING FEEDBACK IN A MORE STRUCTURED WAY THROUGH A 360-DEGREE FEEDBACK INSTRUMENT:

The 360-degree feedback instruments (forms) are favorite tools because individuals can obtain anonymous written feedback from bosses, peers, subordinates, and customers. Because the forms are anonymous, there is little fear of reprisal.

1. Expect to experience some shock and anger when you review the feedback forms. Tell yourself this reaction is normal, as is telling yourself something along the lines of "But I'm trying my hardest and my intentions are pure!" Don't act on your impulse to find out who said what and seek retribution; this impulse will pass. Come to terms with the fact that you're not perfect, and that there are some areas in which people would like you to change.

2. Identify the five items with the highest scores and the five with the lowest scores on the feedback form.

3. On a flip chart under the heading of strengths, list the top five items. Under the heading of areas for improvement, list the five with the lowest scores.

4. Call your direct reports together for a meeting. First, thank them for taking the time to complete the feedback forms. Tell them that you learned a lot from the data and that you truly want to improve your leadership. The purpose of this meeting is to share your feedback with them, allowing them to provide more details and to share your action plan for improvement. Let them know that you will not ask them who said what. Your aim is not retribution but improvement. Begin by discussing your top five scores, your strengths. Ask them for comments and specifics. Feel free to expand on what you learned about your strengths. What was consistent with how you see yourself? What surprised you? Next, share your five lowest scores. Take each item and disclose what it means to you and what you learned about yourself from the item. If you are really feeling brave, ask them what else they would add. Last, share any preliminary ideas or actions that you will take. Ask your people what else they would like you to do. If you don't think your people will be forthcoming or comfortable discussing these issues in your presence (which is a problem in and of itself), tell them you will leave the room. In your absence, they should generate a list of things they would

like you to do differently. After they have completed this, come back and ask one of them to explain what they came up with. Commit to those actions that you feel you can implement. Whichever approach you take, thank the group again for their time. Let them know your plan and time line to follow up with them and ask how you are progressing. You can use the same process with your peers, either in a group setting or one-on-one.

Three to six months later, call the group together (or send out a survey via e-mail) to follow up:

Items You Agreed to Improve	Improvement Seen?
1.	Yes No
2.	Yes No
3.	Yes No
4.	Yes No
5.	Yes No
Comments:	

IV.   TAKE IT TO TONY'S LEVEL.

1. Call your group together over a lunch of pizza or spaghetti
2. Tell them they have 20 minutes and only 20 minutes, now, to your face (not to each other or to other people) to let you know everything you are doing wrong and everything they want you to do differently. Tell them this is their chance to get all their gripes, great ideas, and provocative points out in the open. If you think it will help, tell them that they won't get any pizza or spaghetti unless they talk straight. At the end of 20 minutes, let them know what you are willing to commit to changing. Do this every few months.

BEING OPEN TO FEEDBACK DOESN'T MEAN BELIEVING EVERY WORD YOU HEAR

The only caution I would offer is that you develop a "false feedback detector." In other words, as you become more receptive to advice and criticism from your people, you also must become more astute about what's valuable and what should be ignored. Letting some things go in one ear and out the other is an adage worth applying in certain situations. If you take all criticism to heart, you'll be devastated. If you follow all the advice you're given, you'll encounter many detours and dead ends. Therefore, filter your feedback; as it comes in, ask yourself if it should be taken seriously or if it should be dismissed. Just being aware that some feedback can be discarded makes it easier to encourage others to give it to you. If you take every piece of feedback as gospel, you'll probably grow to hate what your people have to tell you and discourage them from telling you anything.

> **TONY'S FEEDBACK AHA!**
> Swallow your pride, swallow the
> feedback, and count to ten.

6

YOU TALKING TO ME?

In a politically correct age and an era of influence (rather than power), leaders often communicate indirectly and through inference. Many executives have a tendency to turn specific commands into general requests or to moderate their criticism to the point that direct reports aren't clear about their mistakes. People are so afraid of stepping on someone else's toes that they end up being overly timid or obscure in their communication. They also may fail to communicate to the right people at the right time, avoiding unpleasant situations by keeping their mouths shut. Some leaders commit the sin of talking too much, attempting to substitute quantity for quality and overwhelming listeners with their verbal barrages.

Tony Soprano commits none of these sins. Though his communication style isn't flawless—at times he can be too direct and intimidating when making a point—it is highly effective in a variety of situations. Many leaders today have moved away from the command-and-control, authoritative style to a softer, consensus-driven approach, and they may well have gone too far in this soft direction. Tony's style is a refreshing change, but he balances his hard-guy stance with empathy and, most important, authenticity. Let's start out by understanding exactly what Tony's style entails.

SAYING WHAT YOU MEAN AND MEANING WHAT YOU SAY

Tony's communication style is marked by the following four positive traits:

1. Directness
2. Empathy
3. Clarity
4. Adaptability

As anyone who has ever watched the show can attest, Tony is not one for long diatribes. He gets right to the point, using as few words as possible to get there. He also uses everyday language—no big words that you have to look up in the dictionary. His guys respect Tony's style because they know he doesn't hold back. If he's upset with them, they know it. He may not always speak elegantly or grammatically—and his expressions can be coarse—but people always know where they stand with him. He also expects others to be concise and get to the point and he can get impatient if the pace is a little slow.

TONY ON HOW TO DELIVER FEEDBACK

"Well, spit it out!"

Many leaders today hide behind their PowerPoint decks, believing that flowery language is needed to convey key points, that in business settings, they need to speak differently or more formally than they ordinarily would. Tony rarely resorts to euphemisms or overly complex language. He would never tell Christopher, "I believe it would be advisable if you were to practice a form of waste disposal on Mr. X to prevent him from articulating unpleasant sentiments."

Tony's communication style can be confrontational at times, but he often is able to avoid the negative fallout of confrontations because of his high level of emotional intelligence. This combination is often disarming (sometimes literally so). Tony reads people's emotions so adroitly (except for Carmela at times) that he can intuit if there's a problem or issue that might be getting in the way of achieving a goal. He uses his instincts to back off from his confrontational style when he sees that it will exacerbate a problem, a technique that gives him the freedom to push people hard so he can get the information he needs. He can sense the point where he needs to back off, and this enables him to keep the pressure on when other bosses might have to let up.

In one of the first episodes, for example, at a famous Tony barbecue, Tony notices that Christopher is a bit quiet. He says to Christopher, "Enough of this shit, what's wrong with you?" At first Christopher does not reply. Tony, however, is undeterred by this reaction and repeats, "I asked you what's wrong?" Reluctantly, Christopher admits that he believes Tony should have handled a situation differently. This is difficult for Christopher to admit, in part because he wants Tony's approval as well as his blessing for a promotion and knows this might not be the best way to go about achieving these goals. Tony, however, is able to elicit the valuable information from Christopher because he's direct, persistent, and genuinely caring. When Tony asks Christopher, "What's wrong with you?" it's not meant only as a criticism but as honest concern regarding Christopher's emotional state. Tony is brilliant at showing his soft side when he's being tough. If Tony were only tough, Christopher would be tempted to withhold information. It's the paradoxical combination of soft and hard that allows Tony to communicate effectively. This represents Tony at his authentic best.

In addition, when Tony has a difficult conversation with someone close to him, he often ends the tough talk with a hug. In this caring physical gesture, Tony is communicating what he feels about the person to temper his harsh words. In every hug he gives, Tony is saying, "It's okay now. We will move forward. I will not hold it against you." This allows him to say things to his people that a less empathetic leader couldn't get away with. Many leaders today opt for soft or hard but don't attempt to find a middle ground between the two. Jerry, for instance, is a top executive with a software company that has been going through some tough times. Jerry has been meeting with the managers of seven different teams to ascertain who in each team should be retained and who should be let go. Understandably, the team leaders don't want to "betray" any team members. Almost every conversation with Jerry starts out with the team leader insisting everyone is indispensable. Though Jerry gently pushes and prods, he clearly communicates through his words and body language that he's not going to nail them if they refuse to provide him with names. As a result, his managers feed him a few token names of people they either don't like or who they know plan to leave the company soon (because of retirement or other job offers). Of course, taking the opposite approach can also have negative consequences. If Jerry had charged into each manager's office and said, "Either you're going to do what I ask right now or your name will be on the top of my 'let go' list," he would have alienated his direct reports. Even worse, they might sabotage the lists they gave him because they resented his heavy-handed approach.

If Tony were given this assignment, he might have slapped around a few reluctant managers who withheld names, but afterward, he would have expertly empathized with their divided loyalties to the point that they didn't hold a grudge against him.

Another trait of Tony's communication style is clarity. Tony is always very clear about what he expects to be done and when the task is to be completed. He does not leave any room for misinterpretation. A classic example is when Brendon and Christopher hijacked one of Junior's trucks after being told not to as a result of a sit-down. When Tony finds out what they've done and clearly isn't pleased, Christopher asks him what to do. Tony replies, "What you are to do is, take the suits and put them back in the truck and then take them back and call my uncle." He finishes with "You leave trucking and everything else that belongs to my uncle alone . . . you got it?" Not only is the task clear but so are the expectations for future operations—no more messing in Junior's operations. For Christopher, the consequences of not obeying are also clear.

Many leaders don't take the time or make the effort to achieve this clarity in their communication. I've worked with otherwise brilliant executives who seem to believe that their direct reports should somehow sense what they're really saying. I remember one instance when a senior vice president was chewing out a project manager because he had delivered a report two days late. The project manager maintained that the vice president had told him that he needed the report by "Wednesday at the latest" and the manager had turned it in Tuesday afternoon. The vice president replied, "What's the matter with you? Can't you read between the lines? Clearly, I implied that I needed the report as soon as possible."

Clearly, he did not. Reading between the lines is not the best technique for communicating important information. Tony is skilled at testing the clarity of people's understanding. For example, Tony brought the twin brother of a man he had whacked over to his crew to keep an eye on him. Paulie tells Tony that he thinks this guy is acting a little strange and may have found out that Tony had his brother killed. When Tony is alone with the brother, he decides to handle the situation with his usual candor by asking the brother, "You got a problem?" Tony waits a few seconds, but there is no response. Rather than walking away from an uncomfortable situation, Tony comes back with, "Well I heard that maybe you got a problem." The brother timidly replies that he has no problem. Tony does not allow this ambiguous response to stand, insisting, "You say you're sure. Don't say you're sure if you're not sure."

Tony's fourth distinctive trait is his ability to adapt his communication style. He recognizes the need to change his tone and demeanor based on whom he's talking to. With Johnny Sack, Carmine's underboss, Tony is a little more formal, showing just a modicum of respect. He uses less profanity and bigger words and makes sure that he enunciates. At the same time, he doesn't give the appearance that he is in any way inferior to Johnny. His manner has just the right amount of respect—not quite that of an equal but definitely not that of a subordinate.

Though Tony also shows respect to Junior, it takes a different form in their communications. Tony carefully chooses his words when talking to his uncle, recognizing how sensitive Junior is to negative feedback. When Tony has to deliver bad news, he moderates his usually direct communication style, couching the bad news in ways that he avoids making Junior defensive or, even worse, causing his uncle to tune him out. At one point, the captains had complained to Tony that Junior wasn't distributing the take fairly, and to help Junior understand this problem, Tony used a metaphor rooted in Roman history to illustrate the issue. Unfortunately, the metaphor goes over Junior's head. Undeterred, Tony tells Junior a story Junior had told him when he was a child. At this point, the message gets through.

These four traits—directness, empathy, clarity, and adaptability—are in short supply in leadership circles. As you read about how Tony uses these traits to be an effective boss, did you find yourself thinking, That sounds like me? Or did his style seem light-years removed from your own? The following exercise will help you assess your style versus Tony's. As you'll see, there are two lists of quotes, each reflecting the communication style of two types of leaders (though the quotes from the Tony-like Boss aren't direct quotes from Tony Soprano but rather how Tony might speak if he were CEO of a major corporation). Place check marks next to the quotes on each list that might reflect something you would say. Add up the check marks for each type of boss and see which one fits you best.

The Tony-like Boss

☐ The deadline is Thursday; there are no extensions or excuses allowed.

☐ If you're having problems with that guy in HR, come to me right away and we'll figure out how to deal with him. I'll take care of him.

☐ I don't want any of you who are losing your jobs in this downsizing to leave this company feeling like we didn't do all we could for you. If you need something, now or a year from now, I expect you to call me.

☐ I want to give you some negative feedback about your performance, and I know it hurts, but I've been there too. So here it is: You gave the Mancuso brothers 5 percent too much. That Joe, he got one over on me the first time we made a deal, too. No one's perfect.

☐ We have to improve performance by 10 percent. Not 8 percent or 9 percent, but 10 percent. To do that, I expect every one of you to put in at least five additional hours per week.

☐ I want to create a partnership with Acme Corporation, but only if they agree to a 50-50 split of all the revenue we generate and as long as our knowledge-exchange program benefits both companies equally.

☐ I know I said that we would only do a 50-50 split with Acme, but I'd take a lower percentage if we could forge an alliance with XYZ Corporation.

☐ Yeah, Joe in sales is a jerk, but he's a very productive jerk and we need him, so I'll treat him like my best friend until he crosses the line.

The Un–Tony-like Boss

☐ It would be great if you could get this to me some time next week.

☐ If you're having problems with that guy in HR, maybe you should just try and steer clear of him.

❏ I'm sorry the downsizing has cost you your jobs, but these are tough times and you're just the unfortunate victims.

❏ Here's the performance feedback, and it's negative, which is very disappointing. You really let me down on this Mancuso deal.

❏ We have to improve performance, so I expect all of you to put in more time, effort, and energy.

❏ I want to create a partnership with Acme, but only if they agree to a fair deal.

❏ I said I would only partner with Acme if they agreed to a fair deal, and I'm sticking to that philosophy regarding XYZ, even though a partnership with them could turn this company around.

❏ Joe in sales may be a high producer, but I refuse to treat him any differently than the worst employee this company has.

If you find that you have more check marks next to the Un–Tony-like than the Tony-like Boss, don't worry. You can acquire more of Tony's communication skills by becoming more aware of what they are and by working on some of the exercises later in this chapter. First, though, you need to get past your fear. Most people are afraid to ask the tough questions because they're afraid of the answers. As a result, they don't ask their direct report what's really bothering her or their alliance partners why they're having second thoughts about a joint venture. They're afraid to hear the answers; they're scared that they'll have to address a highly emotional issue with the direct report or that they may have to put the brakes on a once-promising joint venture. They're also afraid they might hear bad news about themselves and have to change their own behavior based on what they hear. Yet once they hear the truth, they are in a much better position to communicate directly, empathetically, clearly and flexibly. The issues that need to be addressed are addressed, and the relationship benefits. If these issues are allowed to simmer below the surface, the relationship won't move forward. When people take refuge in generalities and vague language, it's a sign that they're avoiding the core issues.

Tony is many things, but one thing he is not is fearful. He is ready to confront whatever comes his way, which is why he communicates so effectively.

DRIVING THE RIGHT COMMUNICATIONS VEHICLE

Some leaders are well informed about what is going on within their organizations and in external environments. They have access to this information in part because they're good communicators but also because they're adept at using different forums and opportunities to communicate with people. These leaders know who's doing well, who's struggling, who's aligned with whom, and who's talking behind others backs. They're the first ones to spot emerging technology trends and market changes because they rely on more than reading the trade papers and the Internet to obtain their information.

Communication in the Soprano family is fluid and ongoing, formal and informal. It's amazing what can be accomplished by phone and regular spaghetti lunches, tequila shots at the strip club, espresso during a breakfast meeting at one of the infamous meat markets, or, of course, dinner at Vesuvios. Tony and his captains recognize that it's not efficient to wade through 50 e-mails or voice mails daily or to sit through numerous three-hour meetings. They also seem to recognize that different forums are useful for different communication goals. At a breakfast meeting at Centannis Meat Market, for instance, Tony asks and gets the lowdown on the Triborough Towers contract. He finds out there is a little bit of trouble and Christopher volunteers to take care of it. This is a great example of how organizations benefit when they have regular, informal meetings. Tony fully expects that by having an ongoing discussion on important topics, someone will step up to the plate and offer good ideas and solutions.

Besides using the meat market, Tony has held meetings at fancy restaurants, dives, strip clubs, cars, his basement, parks, alleys, retail establishments, the racetrack, and at many other venues. Many times, the medium fits the message; he talks about a horse deal at the racetrack and a real estate deal on a vacant parcel of land. When one of Tony's "clients," a gambler who just happens to be a doctor with an HMO, can't pay his debt, Tony hatches a scheme at the strip club to defraud the HMO. The settings lend themselves to a discussion of specific issues, creating an ambience that encourages enthusiasm and specificity.

No matter where these meetings are held, the atmosphere is always one of candor and openness. The captains admit when they fuck up and take accountability for their operations. The focus is on moving forward and finding solutions. Tony may get upset at something they did but would rather hear it from the "guilty" party rather than not hear it at all or, worse yet, hear it from someone else.

These "meetings" are also important vehicles to get the buzz on other family members. At this same meeting at Centannis, Silvio tells Tony about some gossip he heard at the club. He says the word on the street is that Junior is going to whack little Pussy in the restaurant owned by Tony's childhood friend, Artie Bucco. Armed with the information, Tony can strategize how to avoid having the hit take place in his friend's restaurant.

Tony also uses informal gatherings to stay connected with his key people and allow them to see his "softer" side. One of the big problems hard-nosed, command-and-control leaders face is being perceived as stiff and impersonal. People feel they can't talk to these leaders outside of a formal meeting, and they don't feel particularly inspired by them because of their ramrod straight demeanor. As a result, relationships between these leaders and their key people are often strained and then their communication is limited and narrowly focused. Tony, on the other hand, entertains his captains on the weekends and during holidays and they huddle around the barbecue gossiping, telling jokes, or comforting each other. In these relaxed settings, they all let their guard down, expose some vulnerability, and ask for advice or help. If you watch Tony during these informal gatherings, he appears to be relaxed but his eyes are alert and observant. Real 360-degree feedback rarely happens within a formal setting. As Tony grasps, it's more likely to occur when his crews have a few drinks in them and are relaxing on lounge chairs.

Unlike many leaders, Tony limits the time he spends in any meeting, whether formal or informal. This is in stark contrast to the typical leader, who, according to various surveys, spends 50 percent to 60 percent of her time in meetings. These surveys also reveal that most of these leaders believe relatively little is accomplished during meeting time.

Wherever Tony meets with others, he usually keeps the number of participants to the absolute minimum. While some leadership theorists eschew these small-group meetings as being overly insular, Tony realizes that these small groups are crucial for getting things accomplished. He understands that small groups of people reach decisions more quickly than larger groups do, but most important, that if you have the right input and the right people at the table, you can make good decisions and move on. Admittedly, large organizations have protocols that require certain types of people to be at certain types of meetings, often resulting in crowds. Some leaders, too, regularly hold large meetings for political reasons, because they don't want to hurt anyone's feelings or out of a desire to obtain a wide range of ideas. In striving for inclusion, involvement, and consensus, though, many leaders have become inefficient at getting the right people in the room to get issues out on the table and resolve them quickly. It's hard to have a meaningful dialogue and get to the heart of an issue with 12 people in a room. Some have accused George W. Bush of relying on a handful of people to make decisions but he has never been criticized at not having made decisions quickly. This is in sharp contrast to Jimmy Carter who was often criticized for having too many people involved and trying to reach consensus too often. Tony's strategy of holding numerous short, small meetings in informal settings makes it possible for him to avoid protocol and consensus-building problems.

Tony is also a big believer in face-to-face communication rather than in the electronic communication that has become a favored tool of many leaders. While these virtual meetings and e-mail certainly have their place, they can easily be overused. Too many managers choose e-mail over personal contact because it's faster and helps people avoid the "messy" emotional exchanges that can come when they're forced to wrestle with difficult topics. That's why more than one leader automatically leaves voice mail for the people who sit in the offices right next to theirs. Even more troubling, many leaders and teams also seem to have forgone the power of informal communication exchanges over coffee, lunch, or dinner. In the era of doing more with less and reducing expenses, we've moved from the extreme of the two-martini lunch to individuals grabbing a quick bite and eating alone at their desks. When colleagues are "breaking bread" together, they are connecting with one another on an individual basis. They are building trust by sharing details of their lives both in and outside the office. They are taking advantage of valuable networking opportunities to stay in the loop about what's going on, what projects are hot, who's in favor, and who's out of favor. People are keeping each other in the know. This investment of time breaks down barriers, builds trust, and helps to establish those relationships that will help get things accomplished in the future. Tony grasps this instinctively; unfortunately, many business bosses do not.

To assess whether you use a diversity of settings/occasions to communicate with people, look at the following list and check the ones that you use as regular meeting places:

- ❑ Restaurants
- ❑ Coffee shops
- ❑ Walks (in the park, around the block, etc.)

❏ Athletic clubs
❏ Sporting events
❏ Bars/pubs
❏ Planes, trains, and automobiles (as well as other forms of transportation)
❏ Poker games
❏ Personal residence
❏ Other people's homes/apartments
❏ Vacation/country houses
❏ Barbecues
❏ Museums
❏ Sports stadiums
❏ Shopping expeditions
❏ Street corners

WHAT WOULD TONY SAY?
How to Put Tony's Approach into Your Own Words

The goal here isn't to duplicate Tony's language and style as much as it is to derive inspiration from it. Obviously, you can't use the f-word in every other sentence or threaten your people with death and dismemberment if they don't meet objectives (though in certain moments, this may be exactly what you feel like doing). Instead, you want to take Tony's directness, empathy, clarity, and adaptability and make it your own.

The following exercise is designed to help you achieve this goal. I've taken some common business situations and suggested what Tony might say if he worked for your company and found himself in these situations. I've followed that with what someone who is indirect, unempathetic, vague, and inflexible might say in these situations. Your job is to find a middle ground that draws inspiration from Tony but scales back his extreme language and actions. After each set of two quotes, write your Tony-inspired quote—what you would say if you possessed Tony's chutzpah (we've supplied a sample quote for you just for the first situation).

Situation #1

You just promoted a highly valued direct report to a new job but the salary approved by your boss is $14,000 less than that of the person who was previously in the position and $10,000 less than that of a comparable position in another division.

What Tony would say. This is bullshit. I know you were paying Joe $74,000 when he was in that job, and I know that Mary is being paid $70,000 for doing the same thing in another division. What are you trying to pull you son of a bitch?

What the Un-Tony would say. I don't mean to complain, but I wonder if this is really fair. Please don't misunderstand me. I recognize that you're under pressure to keep down costs, so if I'm out of line, please tell me, but if it's at all possible—and it may not be—I hope you'll consider increasing the salary by $14,000. Of course, if that's too much, than any increase would be much appreciated.

What you would say. Look, do you want to risk losing someone who has helped our team exceed its goals by more than 20 percent over the past two years? Because if I'm forced to offer him the salary you're proposing, he's going to be insulted and look for a job, and I wouldn't blame him. To avoid that possibility, we need to give him a sizable increase—at least $10,000.

Situation #2

You hear from a colleague in another group that one of your direct reports, Julio, has been criticizing your leadership style behind your back. He's been complaining to the CEO that you've lost the respect of some members of your team because you've been pushing them too hard without putting in the same amount of time yourself.

What Tony would say. Julio, I've been hearing that you have a problem with me, that you went to the CEO to complain about how I've been running my group. Do you understand how that doesn't sit right with me? Maybe this will help you understand. What if I went to the CEO and told him how you and Norma in accounting have been seeing each other? Considering his policy—not to mention the fact that you're married to the CEO's fuckin' sister—I don't think it would go over real well. So why don't you just tell the CEO you heard wrong and next time you feel the urge to spill your guts, you come to me first.

What the Un-Tony would say. Julio, I was disturbed to hear that you said something negative about me to the CEO. Perhaps I have it wrong and it wasn't negative at all—and if that's the case, I apologize—but perhaps we can talk about it? It may have been unintentional, but if the comments were indeed negative, I'm concerned about the effect it will have on my career. I also trust that in the future, you'll come to me first with any problems before you go to the CEO.

What would you say?

Situation #3

You're attempting to renegotiate terms with a key supplier and you want to impress on them the concept of partnering. From your end, that means that you'll make them your exclusive supplier, resulting in a greater sales volume. From their end, it means being more flexible and responsive when your company needs something. You sense they're reluctant to enter into this partnership arrangement and you need to convince them that it's a good idea.

What Tony would say. Look, I understand your concerns. You're thinking, Is this going to mean more work and less money for us; how do we know you'll keep your word? You don't. But we don't know if you'll keep your word to be more responsive and flexible. It's a matter of trust. So I'm asking you: Do you trust me? 'Cause if you do, then you've got nothing to worry about.

What the Un-Tony would say. Please consider our proposition with the utmost seriousness. It's tremendously important for our organization to establish partnering relationships with our vendors. It will allow us to achieve our goals as a knowledge company. This isn't some idea that we just came up with but the result of over a year of planning and study. We know these partnering relationships are the wave of the future, and we're extending you an invitation to be part of that future.

What would you say?

MONITORING DEVICES
Watch What You Say

Becoming a direct, empathetic, clear, and adaptable communicator is a gradual process, and to facilitate this process requires continuous awareness. You need to pay attention to your communication style and methods and compare and contrast them with Tony's style and methods. To that end, I've included some monitoring devices that will help you in this regard.

First, here are a series of questions you can ask yourself to determine your progress:

The Talking the Talk Quiz

How often have you:

1. Said what you really wanted to say (rather than what was politically correct or designed to ease tensions)?
   Yes/most of the time _____   No/wimped out _____

2. Discussed an idea without a PowerPoint presentation?
   Yes/most of the time _____   No/wimped out _____

3. Let the other person know you were angry or upset?
   Yes/most of the time _____   No/wimped out _____

4. Gave clear instructions/requests?
   Yes/most of the time _____   No/wimped out _____

5. Communicated the consequences of not delivering?
   Yes/most of the time _____   No/wimped out _____

6. Laid out what was acceptable and unacceptable performance?
   Yes/most of the time _____   No/wimped out _____

7. Had informal chat time with colleagues or subordinates?
   Yes/most of the time _____   No/wimped out _____

8. Used your insight into how someone else was feeling to build a relationship?
   Yes/most of the time _____   No/wimped out _____

9. Changed the way you talked to someone based on your knowledge of his or her needs/requirements?
   Yes/most of the time _____   No/wimped out _____

10. Relied on simple words and straight talk to get your points across?
    Yes/most of the time _____   No/wimped out _____

SCORING (based on number of Yes answers):

0–2: Personna non gratta

3–5: Foot soldier

6–8: Captain

8–10: Boss of bosses

The next monitoring exercise is a checklist of mistakes you want to avoid if you want to demonstrate Soprano-style communication skills:

Mistake #1: Talking like a mealymouthed weasel who's afraid that whatever he says is going to bite him on the butt.

Mistake #2: Using $100 words that sound great but no one else has a fuckin' clue what you're talking about.

Mistake #3: Giving speeches like you're some kind of professor instead of asking questions like you're a regular guy.

Mistake #4: Forgetting that just 'cause you know what you want doesn't mean they know what you want.

Mistake #5: Not telling people what they'll get if they do it right and what they'll get if they do it wrong.

Mistake #6: Avoiding getting together with your people outside of work and treating them like they don't exist unless there's fluorescent light shining on their heads.

Mistake #7: Telling your guys you don't want to hear what you did wrong; you just want them to make it right.

The last monitoring device involves remembering that Tony only serves as a leadership model, and that all models can be abused if applied rigidly. Therefore, guard against becoming too Tony-like by watching for the following red flags:

- You find yourself punctuating your letters, speeches, and e-mails with colorful though offensive profanity.
- You are so forceful that people look at you in the same way as they did at the junior-high bully who demanded their lunch money.

- You're so candid that you cause people to blush and weep.
- You become so adroit at manipulation that your people start calling you Mr. Machiavelli.
- You go for the jugular when a slight flesh wound would get your point across.

COMMUNICATION TECHNIQUES VERSUS COMMUNICATION PERSONALITY

Tony has a distinct personality, which impacts the way he communicates. His Jersey accent, his pugnacious demeanor, and his wise-guy attitude all contribute to how he makes his points. It would obviously be ludicrous for you to adopt this accent, demeanor, and attitude. Instead, you can maintain your own personal way of communicating but add Tony's positive communication traits into the mix. Focus on how you can be more direct, empathetic, clear, and adaptable in one-on-one conversations and when you're presenting. You'll find that you're perfectly able to assimilate these traits without threatening to break someone's kneecaps.

> ### TONY'S COMMUNICATION AHA!
> Sometimes you gotta use the stick, sometimes you gotta use the carrot, but you always gotta know which is which.

7

TEN TOUGH CHOICES

What We Can Learn from Tony's Most Challenging Decisions

The leaders who make the best decisions aren't necessarily the ones who are the smartest or the best informed. Instead, they seem to possess a knack for making the right decision at the right time. They aren't seized with analysis paralysis when tough choices land on their plates, and they're willing to make risky decisions if the potential rewards justify making them. Though they make some bad decisions, their good ones far outweigh the bad ones. More often than not, these great decision makers rise quickly to top positions in organizations, for this is an increasingly prized skill in a world where decisions grow more difficult by the day.

Like any prized skill, a wide range of knowledge and training has emerged around decision making. If you want to become a better decision maker, you have numerous learning options. You can sign up for all types of courses that provide you with decision-making techniques, from formal option analysis to more creative, intuitive approaches. I've found, however, that the best decision makers tend to follow certain models, whether consciously or not.

Perhaps they had a mentor who provided them with insights about how to make great choices. Perhaps they studied great leaders in history and how they made wise decisions.

Tony provides us with a valuable decision-making model. He's made many difficult choices. Though his decisions haven't always turned out perfectly, he has made many astonishingly smart choices. By examining the ten most difficult decisions he's made over the past four years, we can learn a lot about everything from generating alternatives to acting quickly and effectively when faced with ambiguous situations. After each choice is described, you'll find specific "lessons learned"—ways to apply Tony's decision-making process to typical business issues. Though Tony decides in ways that aren't like many business leaders, given the disastrous choices that many top executives have made recently, it might be time to look at a fresh approach to decision making.

TONY ON THE VALUE OF MAKING A CLEAR CHOICE

"More is lost by indecision than
by a wrong decision."

TONY'S TOP TEN MOST DIFFICULT DECISIONS

10. Whether to Give In to Carmine's Demands on the HUD Deal

The HUD deal was arranged through Assemblyman Zellman, a mutual contact of Tony and Carmine, though it was Tony's brainchild. Carmine, however, believed that his relationship with Zellman justified a cut, and he told Tony he wanted 40 percent. Tony offered him a much lower percentage. Both locked into their positions, and the tension began to build. As the prospect of war between Carmine's and Tony's groups seemed more likely, Tony had to decide whether to give in to Carmine's demands. Another leader might have assessed the situation and determined that it was foolhardy risking everything over a deal in which they both could make money. On paper, at least, Carmine has more clout than Tony. It was as if a junior vice president refused to fulfill a request of a senior vice president. It would have been simple for Tony to take the easy way out and give Carmine what he wanted or at least try to find a compromise percentage that would have made him happy.

Instead, Tony decided he would rather go to war than give in to Carmine's unfair demands. At first, this might seem like an unwise decision, that Tony reacted emotionally rather than intellectually. With hindsight, though, we can see that Tony assessed the situation with lightning speed and determined that he was in a position to win the war of nerves. When Carmine closed the Esplanade operation, depriving them both of revenue, Tony knew that his business was more diversified than Carmine's, putting him in a better position to wait out the closing.

Just as significantly, Tony kept his cool despite his anger at Carmine. In fact, after making the decision, he said, "I'm not going to go ballistic." Like other great decision makers, Tony was aware that his actions would help determine if his decision was the right one. While Tony took some small, retaliatory jabs at Carmine, he never did anything major that would provoke an all-out war. He even tried to work through Carmine's son in Florida to resolve their dispute. Though this attempt at resolution failed, Tony communicated to Carmine through this gesture that he wanted to reconcile. This conciliatory gesture no doubt was calculated; Tony probably figured that it would cool down Carmine. In addition, Tony didn't act rashly as the stalemate dragged on. He consulted his crew a number of times to gather information and make sure he had his crew's support. If he had to adjust his position along the way, he could have, but the information and support he received allowed him to stick to his decision. Eventually, Carmine gave in and accepted a smaller piece of the action from Tony.

What we can learn from this decision:

- **Decisions that flow from strongly held beliefs give you the moral high ground.** Tony communicated the depth of his conviction that he was in the right both to Carmine and to his own people. Carmine, who was clearly operating out of greed, couldn't take the moral high ground. Tony's position gave him an advantage for he was convinced he was fighting for something more than money, and because of this belief, Carmine knew that Tony wasn't going to give in.

- **Analyze the other person's position as well as your own.** Too many leaders focus exclusively on their group's or company's situation and make decisions only from that standpoint. Everyone talks about win-win deals, but it's tough to structure those deals unless you know what the other side considers a win. How is your decision going to impact the vendor you're hiring or the company you're partnering with? How is your decision going to change a customer's business? Tony made the right decision because he sized up Carmine's situation and knew exactly what would happen if they locked horns on the HUD deal. In typical Tony fashion, he was thinking a few moves ahead and Carmine's actions never seemed to surprise or throw him.

- **Monitor the impact of your decision.** Tony was especially vigilant about seeking feedback from his people about the repercussions of spurning Carmine's request for a 40 percent cut. In this way, he could change his course of action if it became necessary. If, for instance, his people told him that Carmine was preparing to go to war, Tony had the option of opening negotiations and heading off a battle. Too often, leaders make decisions and that's that. They aren't willing to adjust their decisions as situations change, in part because they're not requesting and receiving information that might cause them to change course. Actively solicit ideas and facts from your people, and you'll be able to follow through on your decisions in a more effective manner.

9. Whether to Clip Carmine

In the world of business, this is akin to angling for your boss's job or beating out a fellow executive for a top position. The rewards are great if you go for it, but so are the risks if you fail. When Johnny grumbled about working for Carmine and suggested it might be better if he were out of the way, Tony had to decide if he should take Johnny up on his suggestion. Tony certainly had a strong motive to get rid of Carmine (Johnny suggested this possibility during the HUD feud) and Johnny's assistance would have been invaluable. Tony went back and forth on this issue, displaying a rare (for Tony) indecisiveness. Ultimately, he decided not to go through with it, earning Johnny's anger and a vow to seek vengeance against Tony for backing out.

Tony's error was acting before thinking. His instinct was to clip Carmine because he would never have a better opportunity, and he was furious with him. He didn't think through the repercussions of killing a boss, and when he did, he realized that it would be bad for business. Fortunately, Tony didn't fall into the trap that snares many leaders: deciding only with the gut. When Tony used his head, he realized that killing Carmine would be bad for business. Still, Tony may have lost an ally in Johnny because of his fickle behavior, and this could spell trouble in the future.

What we can learn from this decision:

- **Just because the time is right for a decision doesn't mean the decision is the right one.** Opportunities present themselves to leaders all the time, but leaders shouldn't seize every opportunity that comes down the pike. No doubt, it's tempting to seize the ones that offer great potential rewards. Tony could almost taste the increased power and de-creased hassles if Carmine were out of the way. By thinking the decision through, however, he correctly judged that no amount of personal satisfaction in clipping Carmine could compensate for lost revenues and lost people.

- **There's nothing people hate more than a fickle leader.** Think about why Johnny was so furious at Tony for backing down from his commitment to help whack Carmine. Johnny's expectations were raised; he must have been dreaming about taking over for Carmine and no longer hav-ing to be at Carmine's beck and call. When rising expecta-tions are dashed by new realities, people are devastated. It's better never to have raised their expectations than to raise them and fail to meet them. Fickle leaders are seen as being insecure, a label that derails careers quickly. Decision rever-sal is appropriate at times—new information can catalyze a reversal—but it alienates people who were positively im-pacted by the first decision and negatively affected by the second. While Tony was right to reverse his decision, he would have been better off if he had decided from the get-go that whacking Carmine was a bad idea.

8. Whether to Promote Christopher or Ralph (or Anyone Else) to Captain

Let's analyze Tony's decision about who to promote to cap-tain after Richie Aprile's untimely (or timely depending on how you look at it) departure created a job opening. Even though Jun-ior supported Ralph and it was well known that Ralph had a solid relationship with Johnny Sack, Tony promoted Gigi, one of his guys. His rationale was that Gigi was a good earner and well respected; he also believed he needed someone he trusted to watch over the Aprile crew. Tony had serious reservations about Ralph, in part because Ralph sometimes failed to keep Tony in the information loop and because Ralph was dealing cocaine and may have been skimming money off the top.

In making this promotion decision, Tony faced a common dilemma: Do you promote a person based solely on his results or do you promote an individual based on his results along with his leadership ability, his values, and what he stands for? As tempting as the "results at any cost" individual is for a results-oriented leader such as Tony, the costs of opting for this type of person can be high. Do you want to communicate to your people through this promotion that the only thing that counts is results? I have worked with many leaders who preach teamwork, cross-boundary behavior and breaking down the silos, and then they promote leaders who are lone rangers and information hoarders. They do so fearing that if they don't promote earners, they'll leave.

Tony, though, didn't struggle with this decision as many business leaders do. Gigi's values were congruent with Tony's, and that made his decision easy. Later, when Ralph beat Tracee the stripper to death, Tony told Ralph that this was an example of the type of behavior that prevented him from receiving the promotion to captain.

I should add, however, that making a promotion decision primarily on congruent values also has a potential downside. For instance, it turned out that Gigi's crew didn't trust or respect him, and that Ralph had whipped the old Aprile crew into great shape. Ralph's strong performance and Gigi's weak one caused Tony to revisit his promotion decision, and he was faced with another dilemma: Should he reverse his old decision and promote Ralph, getting a top earner in place but also risking being viewed as indecisive and dismissive of his cherished values. When Gigi died of a heart attack, Tony had no choice but to promote Ralph for there was no other real successor ready to take on the role.

What we can learn from this decision:

- **Values and results are both important factors in promotion decisions.** This is another delicate balance for leaders, and a given decision may tip more in one direction than the other, depending on specific circumstances. Tony made a wise decision in adhering to his values in this situation, even though Gigi wasn't an ideal candidate. Promoting Ralph over Gigi would have sent the wrong message to Tony's people, potentially destroying the strong code of beliefs and values he'd worked hard to establish. Ideally, Tony would have groomed a candidate for the position with congruent values as well as an ability to earn money and respect from his crew. In most instances, though, leaders need to take both factors into consideration to select the right candidate for promotion.
- **Back up promotion choices with supporting actions.** Decisions are often only as good as the support that the decision maker gives them. In other words, Gigi might have done a better job if Tony had provided Gigi with some coaching about how to be a good captain and how to handle Ralph. He might have also created some negative consequences for Ralph if he failed to support Gigi. I've seen too many leaders make promotion decisions and allow good people to fail because they didn't provide them with information, coaching, ideas, and other supporting staff to help ease the transition to the new position. Analyzing how and where a new promotee is likely to fail will tell you exactly what you need to do to help her avoid this failure.

7. Whether Christopher Should Be a Made Man and Tony's Heir Apparent

This was both a promotion and a succession decision, and it was a tough one for Tony because of his obvious affection for

Christopher and Christopher's obvious flaws. Christopher had been complaining that he should have been "made" since his work on the Triborough Towers job. Tony responded with feedback to Christopher that he did not take accountability for his actions (there were always excuses) and he still needed to develop his leadership skills (remember the hijacking of Junior's trucks).

This is a common leadership decision-making point. You have an ambitious high potential that thinks she is ready to take on more responsibility and be promoted to the next level, but you don't feel she is quite ready yet. You don't want to lose her, but you don't want to throw her in over her head. Tony did exactly the right thing by providing Christopher with objective feedback and telling him what he needs to do to deserve made-man status. Still, it's a problem when someone like Christopher is chomping at the bit to move up. I've seen people talk their bosses into promoting them, using everything from veiled threats to leave to guilt-inducing pleas to convince their bosses to give them what they want. In some instances, this decision needs to be made intuitively. Some direct reports are on the cusp, and no pen-and-paper assessment tool will tell you if they're ready. At times, this decision has to be made by instinct. Tony seemed to have sensed that Christopher needed more time, and in retrospect, this was the right decision.

What we can learn from this decision:

- **Rely on your gut regarding certain people decisions (especially when you know the people well).** While overly relying on intuition can get you in trouble, here it makes sense. There are times when you're damned if you do and damned if you don't, and besides tossing a coin in the air, your gut is your best guide. When the decision involves someone you know really well, your instincts come in handy. Based on your knowledge of this person and your awareness of what a particular job entails, you can pretty accurately guess whether he can handle it. This is a good barometer, as opposed to allowing your direct report to talk you into the promotion. It's easy to feel guilty when your direct report comes to you with a sad, disappointed look and implies that you let him down. It's also easy to imagine scenarios where your failure to promote someone pushes him to take another job offer and you lose a budding star. As easy as it is to give in to this feeling of guilt and this fear, you should realize that resisting it is often a better option.

6. Whether Tony Should Interfere with a Mob Hit to Help a Friend

This was one of the first big decisions that Tony had to make in his leadership role. He learned that Junior was going to knock off little Pussy at Artie Bucco's restaurant. He knew that having a hit there would be bad for Artie's business, and because Artie was a friend and Tony placed great value on friendship, he wanted to help Artie. He tried to convince Junior to consider other alternatives, but Junior did not want to take orders from Tony and told him, "You may run North Jersey but you don't run your Uncle Junior." Tony sought counsel from Hesh who came up with a great idea to get Artie out of town for a few weeks, but Tony's scheme of a free cruise for Artie and his wife, Charmaine, failed when she wouldn't allow Artie to accept a gift from a mobster. Tony finally came up with an out-of-the-box alternative: torching the restaurant. Tony reasoned that a fire would prevent a hit at the restaurant and Artie could collect the insurance money.

One of Tony's strengths as a decision maker is his willingness to explore alternatives. At first, Tony attempted to stop Artie from being hurt by appealing to Junior. When that didn't work, he went to Hesh, received good input, and tried to make Hesh's idea work. When this failed, he generated his own solution. Tony didn't lock into a decision and give up when his first option fizzled. Some leaders make a decision and become so discouraged when something goes wrong that they want to distance themselves from it. Tony, on the other hand, explored alternatives and that lead him toward his out-of-the-box solution.

What we can learn from Tony's decision:

- **When at first you don't succeed, try, try again.** This adage has particular relevance for leaders confronting issues they feel strongly about. Tony was acting out of friendship for Artie. In other words, it's not a "small" decision when he determined he's going to thwart Junior's plan for a hit. When decisions are meaningful, leaders need to spend the time and exhibit the patience that exploring alternatives demands. It's interesting to note that Tony's decisions became progressively more creative. He started out with the rather obvious alternative of talking to Junior; Hesh's scheme was more imaginative; and Tony's idea of torching the restaurant really is out of the box. Some of the best decisions I've seen leaders make come after the first two or three (or more) options didn't work. Small, controlled failure energizes proud leaders, causing them to work harder and more creatively to come up with solutions.

5. Whether to Have Meadow's Soccer Coach Killed

Tony and Carmela found out that Meadow's soccer coach had been having sex with Meadow's friend and soccer teammate. This was the same guy they initially thought was the greatest; Tony had used bribery and intimidation to get him to stay on as coach. After the discovery of his sexual abuse, Tony and the guys decided to kill him. To these men abusing a minor girl violated every code in their book. At first no one (except Meadow) had any objections to Tony taking action. Then Tony talked to Dr. Melfi about this situation, and she recommended letting the judicial system punish the coach. More important, she asked Tony why he "always has to be the one to set things right."

TONY ON THE IMPORTANCE OF ANALYZING
THE RAMIFICATIONS OF A HIT
"I don't want to create confusion and
insubordination."

Tony was still hell-bent on killing the coach until Artie questioned the advisability of this action. He talked about how killing the coach was wrong and that the only thing it would accomplish would be making them feel better. Tony ended up getting drunk and decided not to go through with the hit.

This is a great example of why it's often not wise to make decisions purely on emotion. I've seen too many top executives embark on programs, policies, and strategies out of anger, pride, and envy. They've made emotional decisions despite the advice of others that they were making bad decisions. Caught up in their emotional momentum, they were either too stubborn to listen or too convinced of the rightness of their position to attach much credence to what others had to say. To his credit, Tony listened.

What we can learn from this decision:

- **Solicit and reflect on a few other opinions before deciding.** Even if you're convinced you're right and that you know exactly what needs to be done, ask a trusted advisor or two for their input, especially in the heat of battle. People who are under pressure and dealing with emotional issues can be convinced they know what to do, but their reasoning may be flawed because of this pressure and emotion. Ideally, you'll solicit more than one other opinion and data from several sources. If only Dr. Melfi or only Artie had told Tony that killing the coach was wrong, he probably would have gone ahead with it. It was the accumulated weight of their separate but concurring opinions that caused him to reconsider his decision. I'm not suggesting that you make all your decisions based on the majority opinion or that you delay decisions to gather opinions from five or ten difference sources. In certain instances, though, it pays to hear what other people have to say and to be sure you are comfortable with the amount of data you have.

- **Expend your emotional energy before you act.** Tony diminished some of his anger and desire for vengeance by talking about what a terrible thing the coach had done. Of course, he didn't say, "That was a terrible thing the coach did," preferring his more colorful and crude North Jersey mode of expression. The key, though, was talking about how he felt. In doing so, his actions were no longer completely determined by his emotions. He gave himself a little room to breathe and think. Getting drunk, too, helped dissipate his anger. While I'm not advocating alcohol as a decision-making tool, I do believe that many leaders would make wiser decisions if they expressed their feelings about a situation before making an irrevocable decision.

4. Whether to Enter into Therapy

Although when we first met Tony he was already in therapy and we had not been privy to the process that Tony went through to reach this decision, we can speculate how he made this choice based on his conversations with Dr. Melfi. Clearly, this was the type of tough decision that all leaders struggle with at some point in their careers. While all business leaders aren't deciding about therapy (at least I'm assuming most of them aren't), they do face equally challenging choices that cause them sleepless nights. That's because these decisions require that they set precedents and break with tradition, enduring scorn and ridicule in the process. They're afraid that their choices might make them appear weak or somehow suspect in the eyes of others.

Tony had to violate the mob's taboo against talking about family business with outsiders. He said to Dr. Melfi, "In my world, this does not go down." He literally risked his life by going into therapy. Just as significantly, Tony had to overcome a cultural taboo against therapy. The old-world Italian culture dictated against seeking help from outsiders—there's the belief that "we can handle things ourselves." Actually, this is a cultural edict found in many ethnic groups; Asians in this country can be distrustful about calling in outsiders such as the police, preferring to deal with problems themselves. Perhaps even more significantly, Tony was not raised in a family where talking about your feelings was encouraged. In fact, the machismo code of conduct calls for hiding your feelings.

When leaders make the decision to break with tradition and risk censure, they usually have conducted a thorough and thoughtful risk analysis and determined that the risk is worth it. In Tony's case, he decided that it was worth risking his life rather than experience more panic attacks. This decision also says quite a bit about the strength of Tony's character and the amount of self-confidence he has. When word gets out that he's seeing a shrink, he did not shy away from his decision but confronted his crew with the facts. He didn't apologize or rationalize his decision, as some leaders do when they're second-guessed by others they work with. Instead, he clearly communicated that it's the right thing for him to do and that it won't affect the business.

What we can learn from this decision:

- **It's worth enduring short-term negative responses to a decision if the long-term gain is significant.** Given the short-term mentality in many organizations, leaders have difficulty justifying this type of decision to themselves. Yet as Tony has discovered, the long-term rewards of therapy have been worth the price he's paid. While he no doubt was uncomfortable talking about this issue with his guys, Tony realized that if he didn't go to therapy, he would probably crack up or at least be functioning well below his capacity. A similar decision in an organization might involve downsizing to ensure the future viability of the company. In the short run, this downsizing leader will feel the heat both internally and externally. In the long run, though, this move might help the company become more financially stable and able to avoid a more significant downsizing in the future.

- **It's important to possess sufficient power and influence to weather the fallout from this type of decision.** When you turn your back on tradition and invite criticism, you need to be prepared for criticism that at best can make you feel lousy and at worst can cost you your job. Therefore, before making the decision, determine whether you're really in a position to go against the grain. Do you have enemies within the organization who will use this decision to ensure your ouster? Do you have powerful supporters who may disagree with your decision but will back you nonetheless? Answering these types of questions will help you determine if now is the time to decide. You may need to wait until you accumulate sufficient power and influence before making this choice.

3. Whether to Move Out of the House

This decision is similar to an executive deciding whether to accept an offer from another company after having spent much of his career with his current employer. Or it's like being faced with an offer of a new position within the organization that requires transporting yourself and your family to another part of the country . . . or to another country. These decisions demand relocation not only physically but emotionally; they require giving up an established workstyle for one that is new and unfamiliar.

Making this type of decision requires what I refer to as "leadership maturity." You need to understand who you are and what you hope to achieve before you can make this type of decision with intelligence and wisdom. It's taken Tony four years to realize that his marriage wasn't working. His realization is due, in part, to his work with Dr. Melfi. Over these four years, Tony had been making more thoughtful and less reflexive decisions. As he got to know himself better, he realized that staying in the house with Carmela was making matters worse. When he moved out, he was even able to admit, "It's better this way." Rather than storming out of the house in a rage—as he might have done earlier—Tony was very adult in his leave-taking, formally bidding farewell to his family.

Tony also faced religious and mob obstacles to leaving Carmela. Many Catholics frown on divorce. Members of the mob think that guys who can't keep it together at home probably can't keep it together on the street. Yet Tony overcame these obstacles because he understood himself and that continuing the marriage on its present terms was not only self-destructive but harmful to his wife and children. He was keenly aware of how much damage he could do when his temper got the best of him, and his relationship with Carmela was at the point when explosive anger was always a possibility.

What we can learn from this decision:

- **Just because something is familiar doesn't mean it's good for you.** People stay in jobs—and in marriages—long past the time that it's good for them or their companies. It's difficult to leave a situation that has become as comfortable as an old shoe. Not only is it difficult to leave a longtime employer, but it's tough to jettison a long-term vendor or change a policy or process that you've relied on for years. Self-awareness is crucial for getting out of long-term relationships that may no longer be working. If you know yourself well, you're aware of whether you're staying in a situation for superficial reasons. You recognize that you're only staying with a particular vendor because you enjoy your monthly lunches; that you're not leaving the company because you've fallen into a pleasant routine; that you're not leaving your spouse because it's been so long since you were on your own. Tony made a difficult but appropriate decision to leave Carmela because the marriage was no longer working, and leaders need to develop the same degree of self-awareness so they know when a particular work relationship has ceased to be satisfying and productive.

2. Whether to Allow Junior the Illusion of Control

After Jackie's death, Tony decided not to take over formal control of the family. Instead, he chose to provide Junior with the illusion of having control. While eating lobsters with his crew, Tony started a dialogue about who will take over after Jackie's death, and everyone nominated him. Clearly, Tony used this discussion as a trial balloon, gauging his level of support before making his decision. He realized that if he made a power grab and took over as the family head, a war with Junior and his allies was likely. Tony wanted to do everything possible to avoid this war, but he also wanted to maintain the control only a leader possesses. Thus, he hit on the scheme of giving Junior the title but reserving the real power for himself.

Many leaders in organizations balk at this type of decision. They're unwilling to sacrifice a certain amount of prestige to keep the peace. For instance, one executive vice president refused to accept his company's offer of a COO position with the promise that he would be promoted to CEO within two years. The board wanted to allow the current CEO a graceful exit, and they promised the vice president that he would quickly assume the major decision-making responsibilities during the transition period. Nonetheless, he refused the offer and said the board had 30 days to name him CEO or he would leave. This touched off a board war that spilled down into the ranks and left the company's top executives angry and divided. The board declined to offer the position to the vice president, who left, and ironically, the CEO had to retire for health reasons within the year.

A true leader like Tony is not only concerned with his personal glory but the organization's success. As much as is possible, he tries to foster both. Don't get me wrong. I don't expect leaders to be selfless and self-sacrificing. Tony, though, found a way to avoid hurting the organization and still maintain real power; he simply sacrificed a little prestige. Tony was also clear about what was important to him; he was more interested in the power and influence than in the title.

What we can learn from this decision:

- **Creative thinking can resolve the conflict between personal goals and organizational interests.** At first glance, the clash between a leader's ambitions and the requirements of the organization seem irreconcilable. If you want to get to the top, you're going to have to push some good people out of the way. If you want to grab the resources necessary to accomplish your group's objective, you're going to have to take resources from another group. In reality, creative solutions to the conflicts can prevent animosity between warring parties as well as exits of talent. The key is to explore alternatives, as Tony did during his lobster meal with the guys. People focus too much on win-lose decisions. Though it's not always possible to have a win-win outcome, brainstorming among smart people can usually produce a decision by which the winner sacrifices a bit and the loser saves face.

1. Whether to Kill Pussy

This was Tony's most difficult and painful decision. He discussed the topic extensively with Paulie and Sil, wrestling with what to do after he heard from Vin that Pussy was "wired for sound." Rather than displaying his usual short fuse, Tony made an effort to collect the facts; he wanted to be sure that he had 100 percent accurate information before he made his decision. Unlike Paulie, who was ready to kill Pussy the moment he heard he was working for the Feds, Tony was methodical in his information gathering and analysis.

TONY ON IF HE SHOULD KILL PUSSY

"This is the most serious effing decision I've ever had to make in my life. I need proof."

The analogy to a business situation is when an executive hears that a direct report has done something that warrants dismissal or at least censure. This may involve something unethical or illegal, or it may be a performance failure of some type. Whatever the cause, good leaders like Tony don't react like Paulie and tell an individual that he's fired. Instead, they go through a dual-level evaluation process. One level involves gathering the facts about the infraction. If the facts support the initial description of the infraction, a leader must go to the second level and evaluate what punishment is appropriate for the crime. In Tony's case, Pussy had violated the most sacred value of the family. He committed the ultimate crime and deserved the ultimate punishment. Tony faced the problem head-on and took the responsibility for the hit on Pussy. Because of Tony's solid relationship with him, this was tough for Tony to do, but it came with the leadership territory.

Still, Tony's assessment process was right on the mark. It could have been that Pussy wasn't wired for sound, that he had been running some scheme to find out what the Feds were doing. Maybe he was simply faking being an informer; he got it into his head to be a double agent and earn Tony's respect for his clever plan. Though this wasn't the case, Tony recognized that it was important to get to the bottom of the situation because other explanations were possible. Making a decision to fire a valued, long-term employee has repercussions throughout an organization. If people view the firing as unjustified, it will have a negative impact on morale. Therefore, due diligence is called for, even when the crime and punishment seem transparently obvious.

What we can learn from this decision:

- **Don't jump the gun.** In other words, don't be so quick to make decisions on important issues because you're reacting emotionally or because you're under great pressure to make a choice. In the business world, leaders are finding that more decisions than ever before aren't black-and-white. Many times, there is no correct answer. This is especially true when it comes to termination decisions. It's far more difficult to fire people today than in years past, and not just for legal reasons. Do you fire someone whose performance has been declining primarily because he's been going through a difficult divorce? Do you terminate a high potential who was caught smoking dope in the men's room? Do you get rid of a potential star because you've discovered he's been interviewing for other jobs? Conducting some fact-finding and talking with the individual involved may change your mind about what to do. You may learn enough to give this person another chance or to even change your own behavior to help this individual grow and develop. Of course, if a direct report has committed an illegal or unethical act, you must thoroughly investigate what took place. If the crime is serious enough, the punishment should fit the crime.

A GUIDE TO MAKING GUTSY CHOICES

In analyzing Tony's top-ten decisions, three key themes emerge that can provide you with a sense of what to consider when you're faced with tough choices. When Tony makes a decision, he:

- Roots it in firmly held beliefs and values.
- Relies on out-of-the-box thinking to find nontraditional solutions.
- Is open to other's ideas and solutions.

What is also evident is Tony's growth as a decision maker through his ongoing self-reflection and learning. Effective leaders understand their decision-making processes. They acknowledge their biases, blind spots, and vulnerabilities. They routinely analyze past decisions and try to learn from them. Admittedly, we are not privy to Tony's journals or his "after-action reviews." However, it seems likely that his awareness of how he makes choices has helped him continuously improve his decision-making process over the years.

Be aware of what goes into your decisions. Trace how you arrived at a particular decision in the recent past and where you went wrong—or why you made savvy choices. Rather than beat yourself up over bad decisions or pat yourself on the back for good ones, go beyond self-approval and disapproval to analysis. You can almost see Tony watch the wheels turn in his brain as he measures a choice. This self-analysis will help you make better choices.

TONY'S DECISION-MAKING AHA!

Choose based on what's in your heart,
but don't be afraid to use your head
and show some imagination.

8

UNDERSTANDING YOUR DEEPER NEED TO KILL THE COMPETITION

Developing self-awareness is vital for leaders today. If you look at any current leadership model, you'll find that this quality is at the top of the list. People who understand their impact on others and who are tuned into their weaknesses as well as their strengths are well suited for demanding leadership roles. In a diverse workplace where managers must exhibit sensitivity and empathy to be effective, the old, cold leadership stereotype is obsolete. Emotional intelligence is a requirement of leadership in the 21st century. Executives have to be keenly aware of who they are and how being who they are might derail their careers.

No doubt, years ago someone in Tony's position could have been effective if he lacked even a smidgen of self-awareness. More so than in the corporate world, a gangland leader could be as insensitive as a two-by-four and perform perfectly well. Though I'm no expert, I suspect that Al Capone was not the world's most self-aware person. Yet times change in all fields, and even in Tony's relatively isolated New Jersey subculture, self-awareness has become important for leadership effectiveness. Tony can't afford to let his emotional problems impact his decision making; he can't permit his paranoia or identity issues to cause him to react inappropriately; he can't allow unresolved issues from his past to affect his relationships with people he does business with. In Tony's organization, as in most corporate cultures, there's no longer much tolerance for the superegotistical leader or the supereccentric one. Both have poor people skills due to their lack of self-awareness, and that's a leadership death sentence in these cultures.

Let's start by describing what a self-aware leader looks like and how Tony is closer to this profile than many so-called enlightened leaders in Fortune 500 companies.

SOME SELF-AWARE LEADERS ARE BORN AND OTHERS ARE MADE

Some individuals are naturally insightful, introspective, and just plain curious about themselves. These people are eager to delve deeply into understanding why they do what they do, to learn from the past so they can deal more effectively with the present. These are also the individuals who do not mind undertaking 360-degree feedback or engaging in discussions about their behavior with others. They enjoy training programs and are open to almost any opportunity to learn and improve their effectiveness. With each situation, they assess what they can learn from it to apply in other situations.

Not everyone, though, is so receptive to introspection and reflection. In fact, many highly skilled individual contributors who have great leadership potential struggle with self-awareness. They can be relentlessly, even perversely, dense when it comes to recognizing their flaws. Organizations often hire executive coaches for high potentials who exhibit behavioral problems related to self-awareness, assuming that if these people become more self-aware, it will catalyze behavioral change. Typically, these individuals don't play well on teams or can't get along with other people in the organization. They may also exhibit problems transitioning to new roles because they can't adapt; they lack the inclination or insight to recognize how and why they have to change.

If someone like Tony (pre–Dr. Melfi) worked for your organization, you would hire an executive coach to help him. He's the classic high potential with various "issues" that threaten to hamper his performance and development. If you were considering bringing in a coach for Tony, you might have your doubts. At first glance, he seems like someone who would resist a coach. After all, he was raised in an environment that didn't value self-reflection or honest discussion of feelings; his mother certainly never seemed to take responsibility for her feelings. Given all this, you wouldn't think Tony would be open to learning about himself. Yet Tony, like some leaders today, recognizes the connection between who he is as a person and how he performs as a professional. Tony's increasing self-awareness over the years is due both to his own efforts to become more conscious of who he is as a person and to Dr. Melfi's excellent coaching.

The process of developing self-awareness often requires a person like Dr. Melfi. We need someone to bounce ideas off of who isn't going to be judgmental. An objective outsider is often in the best position to challenge our notions of who we are, and a trained coach is often in the best position to orchestrate changes. You may be able to find someone in your organization to fill this role, but it must be someone who isn't simply going to tell you what you want to hear. Think about what would have happened if Tony went to Junior and was brutally honest about his blackouts and self-doubt. Junior would have had him hit in the blink of an eye.

To develop self-awareness, you need to hold a mirror in front of yourself that gives you a clear picture of who you are and how your attitudes and actions impact others. Executive coaches go about this mirroring process by soliciting feedback about you from your boss, subordinates, peers, customers, and even family members. They will work with you to understand the patterns of this behavior and how it's helping or hurting others in your organization. They may also help you examine the origins of this behavior, assuming that if you deal with the underlying issues from your past you can better manage the current negative behaviors these issues have produced. For example, it is not surprising to see a leader who relies on threats to drive workplace performance come from a home where spanking and strong discipline was the norm.

TONY ON ACKNOWLEDGING HOW ONE'S PAST IMPACTS ONE'S PRESENT BEHAVIOR

"I'm a fat fuckin' crook from New Jersey."

Whether you have access to an executive coach or want to develop self-awareness on your own, you need to hold this mirror in front of you and examine your flaws and strengths without blinking. This means accepting some hard truths about yourself as a person and as a leader. Think about some of the hard truths Tony has come to accept over the years. For instance, he recognizes that others often view him as highly manipulative. He also comes to accept that he's prone to panic, not an easy truth for a macho guy like Tony.

I'd like you to consider the truths that you might have to confront as you gain self-awareness. The following are some sample truths that leaders discover about themselves when they work with executive coaches. Think about these truths and see if you suspect any of them apply to you:

❑ I sometimes come off as a blowhard, trying to impress my people with my experience and expertise because underneath I feel insecure about my position in a changing environment.

❑ People are reluctant to tell me the truth because I bite off their heads when they give me bad news.

❑ I've achieved my leadership position because I'm a great individual contributor and not because I'm a particularly good manager or communicator.

❑ I don't work well with people who are different from me; I tend to work well with an inner circle of like-minded managers and avoid people with different ideas and from different backgrounds. This may be because of my upbringing and education—I've been around white, upper-middle-class people all my life.

❑ I'm a pleaser. I'll go to great lengths to make my bosses and customers happy and to avoid being critical of my direct reports. There have been times when my people have messed up and I've been so gentle in my criticism that they probably didn't even realize they did anything wrong. I want everyone to like me.

❑ At times, my arrogance blinds me to what's really going on around me. I really believe I have a handle on situations, but deep down I realize I'm afraid to ask questions and appear like I'm ignorant.

❑ Though I like to think of myself as a good relationship builder, I realize I only build superficial relationships because it's difficult for me to trust anyone. My mom married and divorced three times before I was 15, and we moved around a lot, and that has made me unwilling to put much trust in anyone. I'm very guarded around people, and I think this causes my direct reports especially to feel wary when I'm around because I keep so much from them. I've been burned one too many times.

❑ I become defensive when someone criticizes my ideas. I immediately focus on fighting back rather than really listening to what the other person is saying and determining if they're right. I couldn't tolerate that my idea wasn't perfect . . . or that I wasn't perfect.

Perhaps these sample truths have triggered your own truths. If so, take a moment and write them down. You may have an epiphany about who you are and how you impact those you work with. It's more likely, though, that you must put in some serious time with your own Dr. Melfi. Let's examine how Dr. Melfi has helped Tony come to terms with who he is and how this knowledge can benefit you.

DON'T TRY THIS ON YOUR OWN
Why You Need an Outsider to Get Inside Your Head

Tony, like most executives, has blind spots, weaknesses, and unconscious motivations that trip him up, causing his otherwise sound decision making to go awry. As much as he might want to, he's not going to be able to identify and resolve these issues on his own. Think about the difficulty of creating self-awareness on your own by focusing on another leader in your company. Choose someone who is bright and successful but who always has problems when he's in certain situations or working with certain people. Perhaps it's someone who invariably gets into confrontations with other leaders when placed on a new team. Perhaps it's a manager who is incredibly knowledgeable about the business and a great strategist but who can't make a major decision to save his soul.

These people aren't deliberately trying to mess up. If they could, they'd stop themselves from always getting into bitter feuds with their peers or consistently screwing up when major decisions must be made. As Tony has discovered, though, people's minds play tricks on them. On a number of shows, he's had dreams and waking fantasies that distort reality. Only when he talks to Dr. Melfi does he realize that these distortions are actually clues to who he is, why he does what he does, and how he might change and become a more effective boss.

I'm not suggesting that you need to see a psychiatrist or even an executive coach. It helps, though, to enlist the help of an insightful friend, colleague, or mentor to give you insights about both your strengths and your weaknesses. What you're looking for is someone who is sufficiently perceptive about who you are and sufficiently honest that she will share her perception with you. This is not self-awareness for self-awareness' sake, but for the sake of being a more effective leader. Let's look at how Tony's work with Dr. Melfi has made him a better leader.

TONY ON HIS AWARENESS OF THE DUALITY THAT GOVERNS OUR THOUGHTS AND ACTIONS

"I find I have to be the sad clown, laughing
on the outside, crying on the inside."

Although Tony entered therapy as a way to stop his recurring panic attacks, he achieved not only that initial goal but he realized other business-related benefits. Tony takes a surprisingly open and flexible view of therapy. Almost intuitively, he recognizes that this isn't a bunch of touchy-feely nonsense but that he can use it. Tony is a highly pragmatic leader, and he quickly grasps that Dr. Melfi's role can be expanded from traditional therapist to a type of "consigliere." For this reason, Tony sometimes uses their sessions to address business issues, sounding her out about his options and how his personal demons and drives might be impacting his decision making. With Dr. Melfi's insights, Tony is able to make connections between disparate ideas that he would have never made on his own.

For instance, when Christopher told Tony that he should have given him praise for his work on the Triborough Towers contract, Tony agrees that he has a point, but adds that he wasn't supported or complimented by his parents, and that impacts how he treats Christopher and others. In a very subtle but effective manner, Tony is sharing his vulnerability with Christopher to assuage Christopher's hurt feelings. Tony's ability to connect how he was parented to how he treats Christopher not only helps his relationship with Christopher but provides him with a red flag that he can raise to avoid this mistake in similar, future situations.

Building strong relationships with a diverse group of people is crucial to leadership today, but many executives are handicapped when it comes to relationship building. A typical top executive with an organization tends to be very good at building only certain types of relationships. For instance, some leaders are terrific when it comes to working with people who share similar backgrounds but are abysmal when it comes to people who traveled different paths. I know one executive who could only relate to people from privileged backgrounds—prep schools, Ivy League colleges, elite training programs—and became arrogant and supercilious with direct reports from more "common" walks of life. There are also managers who are very good at relating up but not good at relating down (or vice versa). And there are those who can relate well to an inner circle but who view everyone else with suspicion and even paranoia.

Many times, it takes an executive coach or another outside viewpoint for these people to become aware that not only are they leading insular work lives but this insularity is hurting their careers and their companies. Certainly these people are dimly aware that they favor their inner circle or specific individuals within their group, but they simply don't see the larger implications of this favoritism. More significant, they don't realize that they need to work consciously at being more inclusive, at establishing common ground with others, and at adapting to the needs of a more diverse constituency. A coach or confidante can drive these points home in compelling ways, offering feedback from others or by leading the person being coached to this self-realization via a series of questions. Dr. Melfi is adept at this questioning technique, and Tony often experiences personal epiphanies because of his answers to Dr. Melfi's questions.

No outside coach or therapist creates this self-awareness overnight. It's an incremental process, and progress is made because small insights begin to accumulate and gather force in people's minds. Since Tony began seeing Dr. Melfi, he has gradually become aware of his flaws and how they impact his decision making. Though he becomes impatient with this process at times, Tony knows that it offers him real benefits. For instance, he has become adept at establishing and maintaining a wide variety of relationships. He has become skilled at managing relationships that are inherently tense, such as the one between himself and his son, AJ. At one point, Tony yelled at AJ and essentially said he was a poor excuse for a son because he wasn't sufficiently tough. Rather than leave the bad blood between them, Tony makes an effort to make amends, recognizing that his hot temper has caused him to say things he really doesn't mean. He brings home pizza, knowing that AJ likes it, and says to him, "Sorry for talking to you the way I did. It was wrong." Taking responsibility for one's actions is a sign of the self-aware individual, and in this instance, it gives Tony the impetus and ability to mend fences with his son. Tony tells his son that when he looks at AJ, he sees himself, that he keeps his feelings inside and reacts without thinking. AJ clearly appreciates Tony's honesty and openness. More than that, AJ relishes that his father is talking to him in a respectful and adult fashion. Without his increased self-awareness, Tony could never have connected with AJ in this way.

Another compelling reason to use therapists or coaches relates to the notion of behavioral change. Many traditional business leaders resist coaching, convinced that they or their people will never change. When confronted with a direct report who stubbornly persists in counterproductive behavior, more than one executive has said, "He'll never change." Therapists and coaches aren't magicians who transform people into their opposites. They do, however, provide the impetus and the techniques for people to adjust aspects of their personalities, and this can make all the difference between being an ineffective and an effective leader. Coaches spend a lot of time teaching new behavior, allowing their clients to practice this behavior and then giving them feedback. By practicing new behavior with a coach, people can often integrate the behavior into their work routines.

Tony, for instance, becomes less of a "control freak" with the help of Dr. Melfi. His willingness to give up some control can be seen in his evolving relationship with Carmela. When he finally grasps that Carmela is serious about splitting up, he realizes that his stubborn refusal to move out of the house is doing more harm than good. Moving out is Tony's way of conceding that his attempt to control this situation has failed. He also stops trying to control and manipulate Carmela through his lies and deceits. For the first time, he is willing to come to terms with the hypocrisy of their relationship, and he and Carmela have a candid talk about their feelings toward each other and the marriage.

Tony also is willing to forgo control in some of his business relationships. Around the same time he has this candid discussion with Carmela, he decides not to clip Carmine, recognizing that this decision may cost him some power and control. In his new self-aware state, however, Tony perceives that losing some power and control may be a better alternative than going through with the hit, for he views Johnny Sack's motives for partnering on the hit as suspect.

Ultimately, though, what Tony gets out of therapy is what every business leader gets out of coaching: the chance to express ideas to and receive advice from a nonjudgmental "outsider." In organizations, people often hold their ideas and emotions close to the vest. When they don't express how they truly feel or think, their "real" persons are hidden from view. They can't develop self-awareness when they're intentionally hiding who they are.

Dr. Melfi lets Tony be himself. With her more than anyone else, he is able to express his greatest fears and his most powerful dreams, and this expression helps him develop and grow as a person and as a leader. In fact, you can see Tony trying to "share" these secret parts of himself with "insiders," and it doesn't work well. When Tony and Carmela are at a restaurant and he tells her for the first time that he is in therapy, she responds, "That's great and it's gutsy." He then goes on about how he "feels his life is out of balance and our existence on this earth is a puzzle." He hopes that Carmela will listen like Dr. Melfi and ask questions that help him further sort through his feelings. Instead Carmela immediately launches into a soliloquy about how her daughter hates her, and Tony quickly returns to his controlling, paternalistic mode. Later, Tony confesses to Hesh that he's been seeing a psychiatrist, hoping that Hesh will provide him with Dr. Melfi–like insights, asking, "What's wrong with me?" Hesh, like Carmela, starts talking about his own problems, and the scene ends with an expressionistic shot, Tony at one end of the room and Hesh at the other, symbolizing the distance between them. The point is that self-awareness can't be fostered by just anyone. Whether you're Tony or a business leader, you need to find someone who listens empathetically, offers wise advice, and doesn't pass judgment.

FINDING YOUR OWN DR. MELFI

To generate self-awareness, the first step is to look for your own version of Dr. Melfi. You may find this person inside your organization—peer coaching or mentoring can be extremely effective—but you should also consider an outside coach. Experienced coaches can often provide the perspective and tools you need, and they can push you in ways that internal people may not be able to push you. Whatever choice you make, remember that you need to find someone you can trust who will assist you with this process of self-discovery. To that end, here are the traits you should be looking for in your Dr. Melfi surrogate:

- Listens well; has the ability to pay attention to you to the exclusion of herself.
- Is willing to ask good, challenging questions.
- Helps you think through issues yourself; doesn't dispense advice unless you ask for it.

- Is trustworthy.
- Accepts you as you are and doesn't pass judgment.
- Isn't trying to change you into something you're not.
- Possesses the skills and perception to help you change the aspects of yourself you want to change.
- Has no personal agenda.
- Cares about you as a person.
- Teaches new approaches and techniques for dealing with difficult situations.
- Provides honest feedback.

Don't make this search more difficult than it has to be. You're not looking for Yoda or Dr. Freud. The individual you choose just needs to be a good, empathetic person who is willing to listen and offer suggestions when appropriate. It's likely that at least one person who fits this description works in your organization, and the odds are you'll have a number of people to choose from.

You can phrase your request for help in any way you choose, but you should be honest about your goal of becoming more aware of how you're perceived in the workplace and how you affect others. Most people will understand this goal and will be glad to grant your request. You don't need to take up that much of their time. Essentially, if they're available to meet with you once or twice a month and are "on call" for emergencies, that should be sufficient.

Once you've identified the person who is going to coach you, you should think about the issues you want to discuss with her. Don't make the mistake of relying on this person for the type of purely business advice you might seek from a boss or the type of ideas you might request from a direct report. This is personal, not business. Or, at least, the purpose is to increase your self-awareness, which means the issues you bring to her should relate to your fears, uncertainties, and other intersections between your personal and professional lives.

The following exercise will help you spot appropriate and inappropriate questions to ask this individual, as well as appropriate and inappropriate responses. The questions will help you determine the types of issues that you should be bringing up to gain self-awareness, and the appropriate responses will guide your search for your own personal Dr. Melfi.

Questions:

Which are appropriate questions? Which are inappropriate?

1. Why do I have such a difficult time confronting poor performers?

2. Why is Donna, my direct report, such a bitch; don't you just hate her?

3. I know that I'm doing a great job and should have been promoted a long time ago, but how come no one else seems to feel this way?

4. Why do I find it difficult to give praise when my people do a good job?

5. I'm completely confused by what happened in that meeting and what I need to do to fix it; why don't you tell me what the right thing to do is?

6. I am afraid I'll make a wrong move and not get ahead; can you help me explore my options?

7. My team doesn't seem to be working well together, and I don't know why. What do you think the problem might be?

8. I don't know if I should fire my direct report for all these screw-ups; do you think he deserves to be fired?

9. Tell me exactly what I should do differently so that my people will perceive me as a kinder, gentler leader.

10. I've reached a pretty high level in the organization by acting a certain way, but I've been told that I need to adapt to the new culture; how can I change in ways that are antithetical to what has brought me so much success?

Appropriate questions: 1, 3, 4, 6, 7, 10

Inappropriate questions: 2, 5, 8, 9

As you may have guessed, questions that call for your advisor to tell you what to do, gossip, or make judgments are inappropriate. As Tony demonstrates, he gets the most out of his sessions with Dr. Melfi when he explores his underlying motivations behind his actions and considers the implications of acting in certain ways. Dr. Melfi encourages him to reflect and understand, and in this way, he learns about himself rather than just learning what he should do. As a result, he grows as a person and as a leader.

Now let's look at responses to a few of the questions to know how your Dr. Melfi should be helping you. I'll list three of the appropriate questions, each followed by an appropriate and an inappropriate response:

1. Why do I have such a difficult time confronting poor performers?

    Appropriate response: Do you think you might hurt his feelings? Do you think he may not like you anymore? Consider your history of dealing with people who let you down; have you ever just flat-out told someone that he wasn't doing a good job and needed to improve? Or is your pattern to avoid confrontations at all costs?

    Inappropriate response: Maybe you have such a tough time confronting poor performers because you're a wimp. Don't deny it. You're afraid of getting yelled at. You've got to toughen up or people will walk all over you.

3. I know that I'm doing a great job and should have been promoted a long time ago, but how come no one else seems to feel this way?

    Appropriate response: How did your parents respond when you did well at school? You may be used to receiving a lot of compliments and encouragement, but sometimes you can do a great job and receive nothing in return. You said no one "seems to feel." It sounds like you're not quite sure. Perhaps you should talk to your boss about your performance and the possibility of a promotion.

Inappropriate response: It sounds like you work for a bunch of ingrates. If they don't recognize what a terrific performer you are, get out of there and join a company that will appreciate you.

7. My team doesn't seem to be working well together, and I don't know why. What do you think the problem might be?

Appropriate response: If you could wave a magic wand and the team could suddenly start working effectively together, what would it be like? Describe how you dream of them functioning together; what specifically would they do that would allow them to work faster, more creatively, and more effectively? When you paint this picture and consider the reality of the team, what's getting in the way? Is it an individual? The team process? Overly ambitious assignments?

Inappropriate response: Teams don't work well together because of personality conflicts. Root them out and you'll see the team get back on track very quickly.

As these responses indicate, your advisor should use a questioning technique to help you think more deeply about the issues you're raising. Remarks that gently push you toward honest reflection are also good. What doesn't work, however, are pronouncements or general recommendations. The pedantic advisor is nothing more than a talking textbook and doesn't facilitate a dialogue that creates self-awareness.

STEPS TOWARD SELF-AWARENESS
How to Achieve a Comfort Level
When You Feel Uncomfortable

As you start asking questions of yourself and examining your motivations, you're going to find yourself operating outside of your comfort zone. Tony's journey to self-awareness brilliantly illuminates the zigzag nature of the journey. After all his work with Dr. Melfi and his introspection, Tony sometimes learns things about himself that make him uncomfortable. For example, Tony realizes one of the root causes of his blackouts is when he's near meat. He suddenly remembers that he first saw his father use violence by chopping off the finger of the butcher who was behind in his loan payment. This is a searing memory, but because he remembers, Tony is able to manage his blackouts.

You should also be aware that you're going to encounter criticism for your willingness to look inward and explore your feelings. In every organization, you'll find people who view self-awareness as irrelevant or who are threatened by those who are open and reflective. You probably know at least a few people in your company who scoff at leaders who think before they act or who are willing to share their weaknesses with others. Even if others don't criticize you, you may criticize yourself. I've known leaders who have been seeing an executive coach, and a number of times during the process they've questioned their own willingness to reveal fears and flaws. They've been conditioned to believe that revealing anything about themselves is taboo.

Consider Tony's conditioning. In Tony's family, expressing feelings (besides anger) was a mortal sin. Revealing secrets could get you killed. When he first starts seeing Dr. Melfi, Tony is worried that if word gets out, he'll be viewed as weak and that this knowledge might give others the impetus to remove him from his position. Over time, Tony voices other self-doubts about his desire to understand why he does what he does. He fears that he doesn't have everything under control—that he may be making a mistake by learning about the "monster" that lurks within. Early on, Tony asks Dr. Melfi, "What happened to Gary Cooper? The strong, silent type? That was an American. He wasn't in touch with his feelin's. He just did what he had to do." In essence, he is questioning why Gary Cooper, a classic hero, could avoid being introspective and he can't. He wants to know why everything has to be so complicated. He questions the validity of therapy and whether it has any practical application in his life.

Many leaders I have worked with think similarly to Tony and harbor doubts about the value of self-awareness, especially as it applies to leadership effectiveness. One leader, a top executive named Jane, viewed coaching with great hostility. Jane's business heroes from a previous generation were similar to Gary Cooper. Though they might not have been the strong, silent types, they were loathe to let anyone they worked with know them well. They also would never admit to spending time reflecting on how their personal demons and desires impacted their leadership or management behavior. As a result, Jane felt that leadership was simply about doing your job to the best of your ability and not having to worry about your emotions or the emotions of others. She was an advocate of leading "naturally"; she said that leadership should be instinctive and not something that you have to work at. Jane was threatened by her emotional makeup, though she didn't realize this fact at first. Consequently, when she finally started working with an executive coach and learning about herself, she fiercely resisted what she learned.

You may also encounter some resistance to self-awareness from people like Jane or from your own internal guardian. At times, Tony, too, runs from his self-discoveries. On more than one occasion, he has told Dr. Melfi he's not going to see her anymore or has furiously denied what he has learned about himself. At the end of the most recent season, Tony has told Dr. Melfi he's finished with therapy, in part because he is having trouble handling his glimpses into the dark night of his soul.

Tony's denial always gets him in trouble; don't fall into this same trap. When Tony is at his best, he is thoughtful and willing to trace his behavior back to the past, sharing experiences with Dr. Melfi that he shares with no one else. He is also very resilient; you should try to develop this same resiliency as you become more aware of who you are and how this impacts those you work with. When something important is revealed—when you experi-

ence an epiphany about why you haven't received a promotion in
the past two years or why you have so much trouble working on a
particular team—keep the following checklist in mind:

- Determine if you automatically denied what you've just
  learned; did you reflexively tell yourself that this couldn't
  be true?
- Ask yourself if you immediately blamed what you learned
  on someone else; did you find a scapegoat for a problem
  that you're responsible for?
- Analyze whether you fell into the trap of dismissing the
  value of self-examination; did what you learn about yourself scare you so much that you found it preferable to dismiss self-awareness as a useful tool?
- Recognize when you're lying to yourself to get rid of uncomfortable feelings; did you dismiss a truth about your behavior because it made you feel so uneasy?

One of the hallmarks of leaders such as Tony is their internal
strength. At his best, he can absorb painful truths about who he
is and use this information to adjust his behavior. He doesn't
become paralyzed by what he learns about himself nor does he
become sidetracked in rage (at least not for long). Instead, he
wrestles with the truths about himself and uses these truths to
become a more effective boss.

I realize that self-awareness isn't always an easy goal for a
leader within an organization. Fortunately, Tony also recognizes
the difficulty of achieving this goal. If he were ever to author a
book called *Tony's Guide to Executive Self-Awareness,* he might
include the following tips.

Introspection ain't for the faint of heart. I'm not a touchy-feely
guy, and getting in touch with your feelings is a lot harder than
getting in touch with your bookie, for instance. Expect to run into
some painful memories and absorb some tough feedback. But

you know what? Self-awareness makes you a more authentic boss, and if there's one thing people respect, it's a boss who isn't a phony.

Don't get down on yourself 'cause you're less perfect than you thought. The more you learn about who you are, the more you'll realize that you fall short in certain areas. This is a tough one. In my life, everybody thinks I have all the answers, and maybe I thought so too, but now I know what I don't know. Because I'm aware of my limits, I can call on others who have the expertise I lack.

Take responsibility for who you are. Instead of facing the truth, you're going to be tempted to shift the blame and make excuses for the messes you create. Don't do it. You want to be a made man in your organization; you got to show that you're a stand-up guy. Whiners, excuse makers, and finger-pointers don't get ahead, and, even worse, they don't learn from their mistakes. Look, I could blame my mother for all my bad traits—she deserves it—but it won't do me any good.

TONY ON THE NEED TO TAKE RESPONSIBILITY FOR ONE'S ACTIONS
"I bring this shit on myself."

Take a blood oath to change. None of this self-awareness stuff is any good unless you do something about it. Just knowing that you beat up on your employees because your father beat up on you isn't worth squat unless you can do something with the knowledge. Maybe understanding that you smack Joey because your pa smacked you will make you more conscious of this tendency, so when Joey screws up an assignment, you won't smack him—or at least you won't smack him so hard.

NO ONE IS SELF-AWARE 24/7

As you may have noticed, there are instances when Tony is as oblivious to his demons and desires as the rest of us. Bosses really need to be "more" self-aware rather than obsessively self-aware. Even with Dr. Melfi's expert help, Tony sometimes backslides and forgets to analyze his motivations for doing something or doesn't recall the triggers that cause him to lose his temper and act in self-destructive ways. Therefore, don't set unrealistic self-awareness goals for yourself. Realistically, you just want to increase your consciousness of why you do what you do. You want to insert mental alarms to remind you to look inward before taking a step outward. Expect to ignore these alarms at times or even not to hear them. In the heat of the moment, self-awareness is easily forgotten. However, just making a commitment to be more self-aware can make a big difference in how you lead. This commitment—which involves finding your own Dr. Melfi—will naturally cause you to be more reflective and self-analytical.

> ## TONY'S SELF-AWARENESS AHA!
> Get control of your demons before they get control of you.

9

ANALYZING TONY

Taking the Best and Leaving the Rest

Even the most ardent fan of Soprano-style leadership recognizes that it's not a flawless style. If you were to adopt Tony's methods religiously, you would end up committing a number of sins that you would pay for, both from business and career standpoints. What I hope you've learned is that Tony Soprano and his organization provide inspiration for a more effective form of leadership rather than a model that you need to mimic.

TONY ON ACKNOWLEDGING HIS WEAKNESSES

"You have bad tendencies, Ralphie, and
I sympathize 'cause I got 'em too."

But how do you separate the wheat from the chaff? Though I've tried to point out the negative aspects of Tony's style, I realize that you may need more help in understanding what makes sense to apply to your organization and what to avoid using. Fortunately, I can provide you with that assistance here. Or rather, I'd like to share the analyses of the well-known consulting firm, Oberprised, Nitpicki & Obvias (ONO). The good people at ONO have looked at Tony's organization and leadership style from top to bottom, and they've generously provided me with insights about strengths and weaknesses. I'll chime in with some of my own analysis as well as suggestions about how you can capitalize on Soprano strengths and avoid the weaknesses. Without further ado, let's examine the ONO report, beginning with strategy.

SOPRANO STRATEGY

Strengths

- Sound business plan
- Diverse portfolio
- Focus on both top and bottom line
- Strong new business pipeline
- Customer focused

Weaknesses

- Lack of vision
- No evidence of three-year plan
- May not be maximizing growth potential in the 35–40 age group

ONO notes that Tony's strategy is smart and pragmatic, but that he comes up a bit short in the vision department. They rave about his new business–generation skills and the quality of his execution, but they cite no less an authority than Carmela as evidence of his shortsightedness. She nagged Tony about the need to plan for the future with some type of investment strategy for her and the kids. The ONO people conclude that Carmela is absolutely right on the money when she warns Tony that if something—God forbid—should happen to him, she and her children would be left high and dry. Tony is very much a present-oriented person, in part because his present is so stressful and action-packed that he has trouble taking a step back and focusing on the future.

My experience is that leaders are either visionary or they are pragmatists. They usually are not both. Martin Luther King Jr. and John F. Kennedy were two of the most visionary leaders of our time but history continues to question their ability to execute, especially Kennedy. Visionary leaders usually surround themselves with detailed-oriented individuals, and pragmatists usually surround themselves with long-term thinkers and planners. Tony would be well advised to develop a three-year plan with projected growth, margin improvement, and perhaps an acquisition or two—maybe it's time to make a move on the New York family. Because Christopher continues to lobby for increased responsibility and Tony seems to want to give it to him, it might make sense for Tony to work on a long-term development plan that would help Christopher grow into his expanded role.

If you're like most people, you resonate to Tony's business and execution skills, but I would caution you to be aware of the downside of his strategic approach. Here are some questions to ask yourself as you start entering new markets and implementing plans and programs:

- Are you moving forward quickly but not sure where you're going to end up; are you so caught up in the excitement of creating new businesses and driving for results that you've lost sight of where you want to take the business in the next few years; do your people understand where you're heading?
- Are you working with an outmoded three-year plan; have you become so wrapped up in killing the competition that you haven't deemed it necessary to figure out if all this killing is really necessary, not to mention cost-effective; have you rationalized not updating the plan, figuring that you're getting so much accomplished that you're bound to be headed in the right direction?

SOPRANO STRUCTURE

Strengths

Current structure:

- Is clear and simple
- Has clear accountabilities
- Is adaptable to changes in the marketplace
- Has strong management processes

Weaknesses

Current structure:

- May not be able to handle increased complexity, especially with more alliances with overseas partners
- Overlapping areas of responsibility in key business lines may cause confusion with expanded operations
- Will need an expanded infrastructure to deal with information

While ONO admires the way in which Tony has pared down his structure to its essence and made it highly responsive to the marketplace, they also are concerned about the structure's inability to function in an expanded or global organization. One consultant archly referred to Tony's structural framework as "Organization 101" and made disparaging remarks about how the basic form of communication is a cell phone and that the structure is so simple that it doesn't even have to be written down. Though I would enjoy watching this consultant give this information to Tony's face, he does have a point. If Tony's organization were to grow, it would have serious difficulties incorporating that growth into the current structure. If, for instance, it was to create more partnerships and projects with groups in Italy and elsewhere, it would encounter a number of difficulties.

First, the structure doesn't clearly assign relationship management responsibilities to any one person, and Tony usually takes on this role. Tony would quickly be overwhelmed if he were trying to manage multiple partnering relationships with groups in other countries; the travel alone would consume huge amounts of time and take him away from his primary management responsibilities in New Jersey. Second, the structure is not geared for the increasing complexity that seems inevitable. As the Soprano family expands its holdings and becomes involved in more legitimate enterprises, it will need a structure that facilitates knowledge sharing and teamwork. To take advantage of the economies of scale and to capitalize on the organization's growing knowledge base, it will need information systems and the type of structure that disseminates this information to the right people at the right time. Right now, it's difficult to imagine a multicountry teleconferencing session involving Tony, Junior, their Italian contacts, and a representative from an organization in a Third World country.

If you're attracted to the simplicity and flexibility of Tony's structure and want to adopt certain elements of it in your group, do the following:

- **Don't fall in love with simplicity for simplicity's sake.** In other words, while trimming the fat and reducing a bloated bureaucracy to its essential elements makes perfect sense, it can also lead to trouble when you're expanding your operations or dealing with complex issues such as global marketing. Some organizational charts need to have more layers than others, just because of the nature of their businesses. Tony has the right idea in keeping reporting lines clean and minimizing layers, but don't simplify in ways that are inappropriate for your particular business.
- **Ask yourself what problems you hope a simplified structure will solve.** Some companies are desperately in need of simplification. Their infrastructures are bloated with duplication in many areas and with byzantine reporting responsibilities. Typically, these complex structures were set up to deal with complex issues, but over time more and more new positions and levels were added and now they're

bloated beyond belief. This is when someone like Tony and his eye for simple, clear structure comes in handy. If, on the other hand, you have a relatively spare structure, you may not benefit greatly if you make it even more spartan.

PEOPLE PRACTICES

Strengths

- Clear link between performance and rewards
- Defined career paths
- Criteria for promotion to capo are understood
- Criteria for becoming a made man are communicated
- Individual jobs appear to be challenging

Weaknesses

- No evidence of an annual performance management process
- Lack of bench strength.
  - — No ready backup for Tony
  - — Who will take over for Ralph who appears to be MIA?
  - — Who are the young up-and-comers in the pipeline?
- No evidence of a plan to build organization capabilities

Here the ONO consulting team identified one of the major flaws in Tony's organization: a lack of attention to talent and talent development. They admit that Tony is a good coach and has done a masterful job in developing Christopher, but Christopher is a long way from being able to take Tony's place as the head of the family. Who else is left, the consultants wonder? How many good years does Paulie have left? Their analysis reveals that leadership of the family does not seem to fit Sil, and Carmine's son from Florida at the helm is an unlikely scenario. They also don't see a logical successor for Ralph and note that if Sean and Matt were evidence of the up-and-comers, Tony is in big trouble.

TONY ON THE NEED FOR SELF-AWARENESS
OF SELF-DESTRUCTIVE TENDENCIES

"I'm my own worst enemy."

Though ONO praised Tony for the way performance is linked with rewards—and how people are generally clear about how well they're doing and if they deserve a promotion—they added that Tony's organization has a cavalier disregard for building human assets. As an example of this disregard, ONO cited what occurred after Gigi suddenly died and Tony had to name someone to replace him. Tony surveyed the pathetic candidates and named Ralph because he was the biggest earner among them, though he was also an individual Tony didn't like and who didn't share Tony's values.

Though Tony builds strong relationships with his people, he doesn't encourage others to build equally solid relationships. The consultants challenged me to name one other relationship builder in Tony's organization, and I couldn't do it. The relationships between Paulie, Christopher, Sil, and Ralph (when he was alive) are weak, and they in turn don't establish their own networks. Instead, they have lackeys who they give orders to. As a result, they don't build the type of trust and diverse set of contacts that leads to exchanges of information and ideas; they also don't create the types of networks that presents them with new opportunities.

ONO's consultants suggested that Tony was on the right track when he brought Furio in from Italy, explaining that Tony went out and recruited and secured a top talent (Annalisa told Tony that Furio was her best employee). He was a young high potential, exactly what Tony's organization needs more of to develop bench strength and to develop its future leaders. ONO criticizes Tony, though, for never developing Furio. Tony used him as muscle and as his driver, and Furio eventually left, ostensibly because he was in love with Carmela. If Furio had been properly developed, however, he might have avoided any involvement with Carmela because he was in love with his job and the way he was being groomed for a leadership position.

Though recruitment and development of talent seem to be Tony's big challenges, he offsets the deficits in these areas because he's such a strong, involved leader. Most executives who take on the type of workload and stress that Tony takes on quickly burn out, and this certainly is a danger for Tony. If he were wise, he would do everything possible to bring Furio back into the fold. He would also recruit with his family's employment brand in mind. What sets the Soprano family apart; what can they offer to hot, young employees that the other families can't? If Tony could answer these questions and recruit with the answers in mind, he'd be in a much better position, both in terms of talent and in terms of his own psyche. It would also help if Tony devoted more time to developing other people besides Christopher. While Paulie and Sil are probably too set in their ways to change, Bobby is a possibility. Tony might want to send him to an executive training program and hire an outside coach to help him recover from his wife's death (which is impacting his work performance).

The consultants also observed that Tony lacks a performance management process, but I don't find this a negative in Tony's case. Performance management processes help people understand what they are accountable for and how they will be rewarded. Tony's group already has clear goals and measures. They get results and then immediately see the reward—cold cash. If they don't earn, they pay the consequences. You do not need a form to make it any clearer. Formal performance management processes are also about ongoing feedback related to how you are doing against your goals. This would be redundant in Tony's operation, for people always know where they stand with Tony; he is a veritable fountain of feedback.

Much more so than the consultants—who aren't aware of how effective Tony's people skills are in areas other than recruitment and development—I believe that Tony provides an excellent model for getting solid performance out of people and creating strong relationships inside and outside of the organization. If you find yourself borrowing from Tony in these areas, my only cautions are these:

- **Put real time and effort into succession planning.** Like Tony, many leaders don't care much about this task. They view succession planning as a largely academic exercise in which human resources puts the names of likely successors in boxes, and these sit on a shelf and grow dusty. Like Tony, you may decide that things change so much, so quickly—people leave, position specs shift—that it's better to decide who should replace whom on the spur of the moment rather than months in advance. In the vast majority of cases this isn't true. Well-managed organizations like General Electric, Avon, Pfizer, and Colgate possess robust talent-development systems where talent review is just as important as the business-planning process. When senior managers regularly review their people and astutely analyze and adjust who is best for a given position—and how to develop people for different assignments—they end up leading a highly effective group of people.

- **Don't assume your people will be with you forever . . . or even for a year.** Tony operates on the assumption that his people aren't contacting headhunters and interviewing for other jobs. He is more likely to be correct than you are if you make a similar assumption. Even though there's been a lot of talk and media stories about the volatility of the workplace and the lack of loyalty to employers, leaders still can't believe that their top people would ever leave them. Believe it. Assuming your people won't leave for another five or ten years fosters a false sense of complacency; it will give you a great excuse to avoid developing successors for key positions. If you have three key people, face the fact that two of them will probably be gone within five years.

ORGANIZATION CLIMATE AND CULTURE

Strengths

- Strong, cohesive team
- Strong values and norms
- Free flow of communication at all levels
- High degree of trust
- High degree of candor and openness

Weaknesses

- Poor/slow response to change
- Signs of employee disloyalty and dissatisfaction
- A tendency to ignore or rationalize problems

Aside from the lack of a formal benefit plan, Tony's organization is a good place to work. As the ONO consulting firm observed, compensation is high, employees are generally enthusiastic and productive, teamwork and camaraderie is excellent, and people feel comfortable enough with each other to express their opinions honestly and without editing. One of the ONO consultants remarked that many companies claim to treat their employees like family, "but Tony Soprano actually makes good on that promise." The Soprano family culture is a strong inducement for people to join and stay with the organization.

On the negative side, the culture seems less stable recently and has experienced trouble accommodating all the changes swirling within the organization and outside of it. Tony seems to be ignoring problems that he should confront, and the results are grumbling in the ranks and signs of disloyalty. The guys are speculating and concerned about what happened to Ralph; they're gossiping about Christopher and his drug problem; they're upset that someone among them is feeding Johnny Sack inside information. As the ONO people correctly observed, Tony must confront each of these issues and resolve them if he wants to restore and maintain the strong Soprano culture.

This is easier said than done. Like any company that is growing and changing, the Soprano family is vulnerable to an increasingly volatile environment and intense competitive pressures. Maintaining a stable culture in this environment is difficult. Still, Tony has made some mistakes that have exacerbated cultural problems. Certainly killing Ralph in a fit of rage was not a good leadership move by any standard. Tony, though, made a bad situation worse by intimating to his guys that Johnny might have hit Ralph. They don't buy his explanation and seem concerned that Tony killed him because they had a disagreement. They're thinking that if Tony could kill Ralph—his biggest and most consistent earner—he could also kill them if they dare to bump up against him. This fear threatens the candor and constant communication that is an essential part of the Soprano culture.

Similarly, Tony appears to be making a mistake, one which all leaders are vulnerable to making: playing favorites. Tony favors Christopher because "[he's] blood, and you can always trust blood," but Christopher has screwed up so much that others in Tony's group are questioning his judgment. When Paulie was in jail and Christopher was the acting capo, Patsy referred to Christopher as a little Napoleon. Sil also gave Tony some feedback that Patsy might be unhappy because he felt passed over and that Tony was favoring Christopher.

I've worked with leaders who once they have decided on a successor, that's it and everyone else's development is forgotten. The stock options and raises go to the successor and even the good performers may be left with nothing or at least much less than they had before. Playing favorites and neglecting your team can only serve to disenfranchise and demotivate.

Tony's willingness to allow questions to linger about the leaks to Johnny Sack is curious. In Tony's organization, this represents a strict breech of the code. You keep your business within your family, and you don't gossip outside the family. It's uncharacteristic of Tony not to get to the bottom of this problem. One would think Tony would have leaned on each member of the family until one of them cracked (Paulie is the guilty party). He must realize how much uncertainty and trepidation this leak is creating.

I'm assuming that despite these mistakes, you find much to admire in Tony's culture, especially the camaraderie he establishes and the open and honest communication. To maintain this type of culture, you'll need to address the following issues:

- **Guard against unfair favoritism.** While a family culture offers many benefits, it also comes with a built-in problem: People get to know each other so well that friendships form and favoritism naturally occurs. As in many families, parents naturally favor one child over another. In organizations, when bosses establish strong relationships with direct reports, one person generally becomes a "teacher's pet." Typically, this is an individual who is a high performer and shares a similar background and work style to the boss. If this individual's rewards and recognition are in line with her performance, favoritism will have a negligible impact on the culture. It's only when rewards and recognition exceed performance—or at least this is the appearance—that people begin to protest and morale falls. Guarding against unfair favoritism is difficult, as Tony's situation demonstrates. Because Christopher is blood and Tony genuinely likes him—and perhaps sees something of himself in him— he assumes that everyone else will share his perspective. In Tony's eyes, Christopher is the chosen one and so deserves more of his time, attention, and generosity. His bias blinds him to how others are perceiving his treatment of Christopher. Therefore, you need to make a conscious effort to ask the following question: Is my successor or favored direct report receiving treatment that's in line with his performance?

- **Deal with problems quickly and openly.** Leaders in close-knit cultures tend to take their people's loyalty for granted;

they forget that candor and openness are the hallmarks of the culture and that if they violate these principles, they can easily lose their key people. Tony is usually brutally honest about most issues, but not about Ralph's death. He underestimates the negative impact his feigned ignorance and misleading statements are having on his crew. He also underestimates the effect his failure to deal with the information leak is having. No doubt, Tony's personal problems—splitting up with Carmela—are affecting his judgment. Otherwise, he would probably be much more up front with his people about these issues.

LEADERSHIP STYLE (OVERALL ASSESSMENT OF TONY SOPRANO)

Strengths

- Charismatic and competent
- Strong business acumen
- High emotional intelligence
- Results-driven

Weaknesses

- Often leads by intimidation
- Volatile
- Most likely a sociopath

While you might not want your daughter to marry Tony or your son to work for him, you might want to hire him to head your organization. A top CEO may not be a particularly good person, but within the confines of the organization, he does good for the organization and the people he works with. ONO tackled the succession issue (assuming Tony would want to succeed Carmine) and analyzed how Tony might fare as a candidate. They determined he was an excellent candidate, but they also raised some red flags.

TONY ON HOW HIS EMOTIONS CAN
NEGATIVELY IMPACT HIS WORK PERFORMANCE

"My temper leads me to make
mistakes in my work."

First, Tony relies heavily on intimidation to get results. The problem, of course, is that while he may use force to generate short-term results, his bullying presence sometimes can discourage people from making long-term commitments or to remain consistently productive. To a certain extent, the negative impact of Tony's intimidating nature is muted by the business he's in; people expect mob leaders to be intimidating. Still, Tony would be an even better leader if he developed a key aspect of emotional intelligence: self-regulation. Too often, his temper gets the better of him and he later regrets his boorish behavior. Tony's typical behavior after his temper flares is to try to make it up to the person with a smile, a heartfelt apology, a piece of jewelry, flowers, or, if none of that works, cash. Sometimes, though, none of this is adequate compensation. In fact, his beating of Assemblyman Zellman over his affair with Tony's ex, Irina, may have cost him dearly. The assemblyman was one of his key contacts and partners in several of his schemes, most notably the Esplanade and the HUD deal. After the beating, the assemblyman broke off with Irina because he was having difficulty "performing." It's likely that no deal or amount of money will make up for this shame and loss.

Leaders can learn to self-regulate and prevent these disruptive behaviors only when they learn what their "triggers" are. For instance, Tony develops a sense of his trigger: he explodes when someone tells him a truth that hits too close to home. In these instances, his usual initial response is to go for the throat. When Carmela tells him their marriage is a sham and she wants him to move out, he smashes the wall instead of her face, thereby limiting the damage. Tony is learning to master a skill of all great leaders: managing your vulnerabilities while simultaneously leveraging your strengths.

As I've pointed out throughout these pages, Tony's style has much to recommend it. His emotional intelligence, his charisma, and his results orientation all may appeal to you. If, however, you see Tony as a good leadership model, you need to do the following as you apply his style in your workplace:

- **Find a push-pull balancing point.** In other words, don't push people around more than you pull them toward the result you want. Though I doubt that you engage in bloody fights with your people, you may well beat them up verbally, especially if you have a hot temper. This may be part of your style, and it may have helped you achieve a certain amount of success. You're known as a tough guy (or gal), and you like that reputation. Realize, though, that the more leadership responsibility you have, the less valuable intimidation is. As you move up the ranks, you'll encounter more high performers who won't be intimidated by you—or who will give as good as they get. Therefore, make an effort to use a wider range of behavior to achieve your team's goals.
- **Practice using the carrot rather than the stick.** Compliment and see if these compliments motivate certain direct reports to work harder and better.
- **Create stronger relationships.** Understand that the more accountable people feel toward you, the harder they'll try to achieve the goals you set.
- **Be aware of what triggers your temper.** If you know what's likely to set you off and make a conscious effort to be vigilant in these situations, you'll probably do a better job of managing your temper and avoiding intimidating behavior.

SO WHAT ARE YOU WAITING FOR
Start Being a More Effective Boss

Armed with Tony's strengths and aware of his weaknesses, you can implement the lessons learned from him in just about any leadership position in any company. I hope you're chomping at the bit to take some feedback in the face or to turn on the charisma. I trust you're puffing on a Tony-like stogie (figuratively speaking, of course) and are ready to confront someone you've been avoiding without fear or second thoughts.

To help you get started the moment you put down this book, I've included a checklist of Tony-inspired actions that are now open to you. These might not be the exact steps you want to take, but I trust that they'll encourage you to take the knowledge you've gained and be a Soprano-style leader.

❑ Level with a customer about why you've missed three deadlines rather than making lame excuses; explain that you discovered a guy in shipping was drinking on the job and is now doing time in the unemployment line; promise you won't miss another deadline; figure that if your customer doesn't appreciate your honesty, forget about it, he wasn't worth having as a customer.

❑ Settle the ongoing "personality conflict" between your two direct reports; knock their heads together (again, figuratively) and let them know you and everyone else are tired of their petty bickering and you won't tolerate it; explain that they either learn to work together or they learn to work somewhere else.

❑ Hold your next meeting at a great restaurant instead of in the grim conference room; use it to build relationships instead of to insert a line of copy into a contract; get to know your people and let them get to know you, recognizing that this is the best employee-retention strategy you could ever come up with short of giving them a million-dollar bonus.

❏ Arrange sit-downs with alliance partners, vendors, and customers to keep things on track and resolve conflicts; stop having bloodless telephone conversations and e-mail exchanges and start using more face-to-face interactions to resolve problems and pursue opportunities.

❏ Set a one-new-business-idea-a-week quota for yourself and your people; make everything fair game for new ideas, from ways to improve the food in the employee cafeteria to great new products and services that the world needs now; don't punish anyone for bad ideas but reward everyone for good ones.

❏ Start acting like yourself rather than playing the part of a leader; allow your idiosyncrasies, dominant personality traits, and greatest strengths as a person to emerge; stop holding inside who you really are and let it out so that when you walk into a room, you, like Tony, will be noticed.

Tony's style inspires people to take these actions. When you meet Tony, your first impression is likely to be that he leads by intimidation. After a little while, though, you realize that there's much more to his leadership style than flexing his muscles. Watching Tony in action and reflecting on how he deals with various problems and opportunities, you realize that he's a much more complex boss than he first appears to be. If you can separate what Tony does for a living from the larger issues he faces, you can see something of your own challenges as a leader. Tony's creativity, courage, and charisma in dealing with these challenges is motivational. Once you move past Tony's flaws, you can take advantage of his strengths.

As a leadership development professional, I've found that people who become superlative bosses often take the road less traveled. Their leadership models aren't always confined to well-known and respected CEOs, but include their martial arts instructor, their high school science teacher, their commanding officer when they were in the service, and their beloved Aunt Agnes. To that list, we can now add Tony Soprano. He may be the last person your board of directors would include in their list of CEO succession candidates, but that's because they'd only concentrate on his flaws. If they looked at this strengths—charisma, vision, the ability to generate huge profits, relationship management skills, and the ability to execute—they would find that his strengths probably match the list of specs better than any other candidate for the job.

> ## TONY'S MORE EFFECTIVE BOSS AHA!
> The best leaders are genuine human beings first and smart businesspeople second.

Chapter 2. Charisma: More Than a Flashy Tie and a Cheap Cigar

Season 2, Episode 9, "From Where to Eternity"

Season 2, Episode 7, "D-Girl"

Chapter 4. Coaching the Poobahs and the Goumbas

Season 1, Episode 8, "The Legend of Tennessee Moltisanti"

Season 3, Episode 3, "Fortunate Son"

Season 1, Episode 2, "46 Long"

Chapter 5. Give It to My Face: Receiving Feedback

Season 1, Episode 4, "Meadowlands"

Season 1, Episode 13, "I Dream of Jeanne Cusamano"

Season 4, Episode 5, "Pie-O-My"

Season 2, Episode 6, "The Happy Wanderer"

Chapter 6. You Talking to Me?

Season 1, Episode 1, "Pilot"

Season 1, Episode 2, "46 Long"

Season 3, Episode 1, "Mr. Ruggerio's Neighborhood"

Chapter 8. Understanding Your Deeper Need to Kill the Competition

Season 1, Episode 1, "Pilot"

Share the message!

Bulk discounts
Discounts start at only 10 copies. Save up to 55% off retail price.

Custom publishing
Private label a cover with your organization's name and logo. Or, tailor information to your needs with a custom pamphlet that highlights specific chapters.

Ancillaries
Workshop outlines, videos, and other products are available on select titles.

Dynamic speakers
Engaging authors are available to share their expertise and insight at your event.

**Call Dearborn Trade Special Sales at 1-800-245-BOOK (2665)
or e-mail trade@dearborn.com**

Dearborn™
Trade Publishing
A **Kaplan Professional** Company